I
am a
Cuban Sandwich
& the Ybor Stories

Mary-Ellen & Richard DiPietra

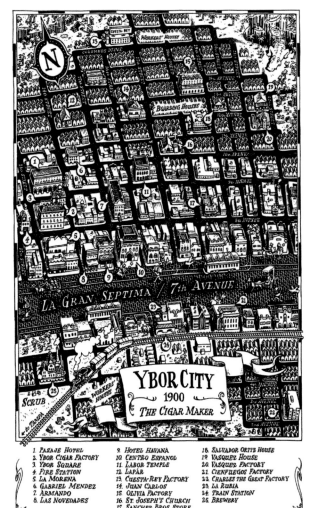

YBOR CITY
1900
THE CIGAR MAKER

I am A Cuban Sandwich

ISBN: 9798613930081

DEDICATION

To
All of us
and all of You
for
Making it Through
This is our edition
of
Gratitude

FORWARD

The great Sicilian author Giuseppe di Lampedusa, in his novel *The Leopard*, a fictionalized portrait of his grandfather, called Sicily the America of antiquity; its people descended from 3,000 years of migrations and invasions that washed across that starkly beautiful volcanic island: Greeks, Romans, Carthaginians, Arabs, Normans, Spaniards, Angevin French. The United States sent the most recent invading army, landing with tanks in 1943, its passage eased by certain people who made sure the shore batteries and local defenders offered almost no resistance to il *Americani*, a large percentage of whom, young men drawn from New York and New Jersey, my father among them, were of Sicilian descent.

This polyglot background likely allowed Sicilians to thrive in America. Strong, quiet, hard-working, proud, aloof, intensely loyal with deep moral feelings, capable of great kindness and heartless cruelty. I don't think it's a coincidence that the Sicilian gangster – a hated and feared figure in the old country – became glamorized in American movies as the dark twin of the strong and silent, also innately violent, Hollywood cowboy. Italians offered deeper, more interesting and complex narrative characters than any found among the Irish, German, and Jewish mobsters who also thrived during Prohibition.

But glamorizing despicable people leaves a mark. Too many Italo-Americans have identified with those antiheroes of power and violence, images drawn from the very people **most** of our ancestors fled Sicily to escape. Too many other Americans, mainstream and ethnic, were thrilled by the ideas of loyalty, vengeance, and respect, the independence and strength presented in the figure of the Sicilian/Italian gangster.

To be Sicilian in America means having to account for horrendous depravity - vile and ridiculous people who are presumed family.

It is hard to write honestly and well about family, for an Italo-American it is nearly impossible – the exposure of dearly loved, intensely private people to the gaze of strangers. The telling of secrets, the illustration of being less an individual than part of something greater – the family – requires tremendous sensitivity and skill. There is a reason why memoirs or fictionalized accounts of 20th century Italo-American social life are few and far between – greatly outnumbered by the family stories of Jewish authors, Bellow and Roth for example, and Protestant Southerners like Faulkner and Conroy.

The first mainstream memoir of Italo-American family life was Jerre Mangione's 1942 classic, *Mount Allegro*, an account of growing up in a Sicilian family in our shared hometown of Rochester, New York. Mangione, a distinguished author and journalist, might be best known today as the uncle of the jazz musician Chuck Mangione. In my family he was remembered as the young man who asked to marry my grandmother's cousin Gina, an offer declined by her parents for his lack of obvious prospects. (An elementary school teacher, Gina never did marry.) Among Italians, a big family makes for a small world.

Richard and Mary Ellen DiPietra have written a big family/small world memoir of Sicilian-American family life on par with Mangione's classic, accomplishing that nearly impossible task of placing their central character, the young Richard, within the context of his broad Italian/Spanish immigrant family, then nesting them all into the rich, lost world of Tampa's Ybor City neighborhood.

Warm and detailed, personally told, laced with mixed feelings of joy and grief, the DiPietras' account stands among the best works in a far-too-small field, a needed reply to the gangster narrative. In it we see thoroughly decent, hard-working immigrants and their many children who honestly embraced the promise of America and in doing so enriched our nation; their lives lived as great and intimate works of art.

-- Joe Gioia

Author, The Guitar and the New World

CONTENTS

NONNO

In the *Pais Vasco,* the *Basque Country,* a small region in the rugged mountains of Northern Spain, a young girl spoke to a young man, words that would change everything. "Yes" She said. Then she did something no one in her tight-knit family had ever done before. She left....for America.

At the same time, a stone mason from Alessandro della Rocca, Sicily had just come over to the states and landed somehow in Kankakee, IL, when he received word from relatives that a new movie house was being built in Tampa, Florida. This grand palace was to be in a Mediterranean design and they were looking for Old World craftsmen who could work in that style. *Nonno,* my grandfather packed up his family and headed south.

The year was 1926 and all over Ybor City workers would gather in the still-dark mornings. My Nonno would be up well before the dawn each day. He would pack a lunch, a jar of coffee, pocketful of cigars and off to work, with his family still snuggled in their beds.

Only the bosses had cars or trucks, so the men would fill wheelbarrows with tools and make the long walk into what would someday be downtown. A small army of Cubans, Sicilians, Spaniards, and men from all over would join together in a long line as they made their way slowly down Nebraska Avenue, across the train tracks, then towards the river.

They would arrive at the site just as the sun began to rise.

Gently they would ease down their burdens for just a few moments and enjoy a quick *café solo* before beginning the days' work. My Sicilian Grandfather was proud and happy to be one of those men. The Tampa Theater remains a landmark to this day.

My dad was Dominic N. DiPietra. Just to give you a hint to the man, the N stood for None. The license bureau insisted he have a middle name so he gave them one, *None*. During WWII he worked as a milkman with Florida Dairy. He was there for 40 years. His route took him throughout

Ybor City, making stops at schools, stores, can companies and mostly, the restaurants. He would cruise right down 7th Ave in his big old milk truck, hitting them all in a row: *Spanish Park, the Columbia, La Tropicana, Cuevos, Silver Ring, Las Novedades.*

Chances are if you got a *café con leche* in Ybor back in the day. My dad brought that milk.

During the summer I would ride along with him on the truck. Instead of any real work I just sat on the big seat next to him. When we got to the restaurants, I was treated like a prince. Everybody knew and loved my dad. At each stop, they'd offer up something special "For the kid." There would be Cuban toast or hot cocoa in the morning, a guava pastry for a snack. For lunch, a Cuban sandwich and, afterward, maybe, a *granita* or a coconut ice cream. For a chubby little kid like me, I tell you it was *La Dolce Vita*!

That's why I could never understand why so many people that I grew up with were always complaining about their childhoods. No matter where you grew up, there were problems. It's tough being part of the working class and that was most of my town. Our shared histories were ones of strife and leaving old ways for new worlds.

In my family, there was never much money. We lived very modestly. My dad worked two jobs, at least, and my mom sewed our clothes. But, man, did we love each other and sure as hell did eat well!

All in all, I lived a charmed life as a boy. Probably, because when I was very young…I met Marilyn Monroe.

JOE AND MARILYN

My godparents, like my Dad were Sicilian and lived right across the street from us in Ybor City. Since they had no children of their own, they were really like a second set of parents to me. Italians have a saying; "Life is too hard to have just one father!"

11

They took me out to dinner with them on special occasions, dressed me up like a pirate for the Gasparilla parade every year, and there was always a new movie to catch at the Tampa Theater. One year when I was little, they took me with them to Redington Beach to stay at the Tides, an upscale resort hotel right on the beach with palm trees, cottages and swimming pools. It was one of *their places*, as they liked to say. Meaning that they went every year and people there knew them by name.

We were in the coffee shop one morning and I remember my godparents were chattering in a couple of languages, all excited, buzzing about something one of the waitresses had told them. It became apparent that *Somebody* was staying in the resort. I really wasn't paying much attention because I had pancakes to finish.

So it was only later, as we were heading out the door that we saw them, Joe and Marilyn. Hand in hand, they're strolling past when my godfather said something to DiMaggio in Sicilian. Joe turned, answering him back in the same language, with his chin and that goofy grin, laughing, just like I'd seen the men in my family do so many times. My godmother was shaking Marilyn's hand and telling her how much they liked her.

Me, I was in this little blue seersucker suit, my Easter outfit and suddenly, she came down to my eye level, touched the lapels of my jacket and said, with *that* voice, "And who is this little man?" "I'm Richard."

"Hello, Richard, I'm Marilyn and this is Joe." I squinted up at DiMaggio. He seemed about 20 feet tall, smiling down at me, hands deep in his pockets.

"How old are you, Richard?" She seemed like she really wanted to know. Intimidated, but not wanting to let her down, I slowly counted out five fingers and held them up.

She looked up at Joe and arched one perfect eyebrow.

I remember her perfume was strong, so strong I nearly lost my head. It was probably Chanel. I know that now but then, I had never smelled anything like that before. It was so…heady, made me feel a little dizzy, kind of like the incense in church when you sat too close at High Mass.

I was a little overwhelmed and began shyly looking down at her feet. She was wearing these black flats and her foot was flexed, so the lining was showing which was shiny like silk and brightly colored with stripes of gold and red and brown. In contrast, her foot was white as marble. I was mesmerized.

Out of a fuzzy dream, I heard "Well, Richard, it was very nice meeting you, Bye, bye." That jolted me out of my reverie and I barely got out a small, "Bye" as they walked away. DiMaggio already had his arm around Marilyn's shoulder and turning her head she threw me one of those brilliant smiles. My godparents were all flustered, "*Bedda Matri!* Can you believe that? "And, they were so nice. What a happy couple!"

I just stood around bewildered, wondering what the hell was that all about! You see, I had no idea then who this person was, but she left me with an idiotic smile on my face for the rest of the week.

It was a daze that would soon work its way into our family mythology, because it was soon after that the *7 Year Itch* came out and Marilyn took off like a rocket.

My mom would love looking through magazines, *Photoplay*, *Life*, and *Look*. She would sometimes order these books of the whole year in review, full of photos and stories. One day, a new book came; there was a 1955 on the cover. I was turning the pages looking for pictures when Holy Crap! Marilyn's in here! And… her dress is all blowing up and you can see her legs and her panties! My mouth went dry; I could feel my little heart hammering away. I needed to inspect this a little further in private. Looking around, I decided. Ah, behind the sofa, perfect! With the book all laid out, I was going through the photos, over and over, when suddenly, the room grew dim and I heard my father's deep voice,

"What the hell are you doing back there?"

13

My Dad llifted me up and took the book saying, "Oh, you shouldn't be looking at this."

"Noooo, it's mine, it's mine", I cried. "She sent it for me!" My dad had a hard time keeping a straight face as he said, "Well, we'll keep it for you until… you're big enough." And, so began a life of woman-worshipping for Richard.

Then came a day, it didn't seem that long afterward. I was walking through the halls of Our Lady of Perpetual Help, with a note in my hand for one the sisters. A rustle of fabric from behind me and Sister Stephanus hurried past stopping at the open doorway and gesturing to the nun in the classroom.

As the sister came out of the door, she leaned over and whispered, "Marilyn Monroe just died!" Both the nuns were stricken. Tears streaming down their faces, they hugged each other, sobbing like little girls. I was shocked and saddened by the news but I still couldn't keep my eyes off the two sisters.

These were young women - not much more than girls, like my three sisters really, with their own emotions and lives outside of this place. I had never thought of them that way before. To me, they'd always been just *Penguins*, humorless and unemotional. Standing there staring with my mouth open, I wasn't even aware that I'd been crying until I looked down and saw the stains of the teardrops that blurred the note in my hand.

 Lost, I turned and bolted down the corridor, sunlight streaming through the doorway at the end. I clanged onto the old metal fire escape. This was where we always came to bang the erasers - watching the clouds of chalk dust drift onto the basketball court below.

Looking blankly down at the street, I could see the corner drug store where we used to hang out, the sounds of pinball drifting up to the second floor. The neighborhood was spread out before me; cigar factories standing tall in the distance, a typical sunny Ybor City day. It just didn't seem as bright as I thought it should be.

Sr. Mary Margaret leaned into the doorway. "Richard,

what are you doing out here?" Head down, I answered with a shrug. Sister tried again, "Did you hear what we were talking about in the hallway?" I nodded, the tears close now. Sister's voice was soft saying, "She's at peace. Come on let's go back inside."

"I can't sister, the note." I replied, showing her the tear-stained page. She comforted me taking the note saying, "I'll take care of that; don't you worry." Sister reached into her sleeve, pulled out a clean white handkerchief and gently wiped my tears. "Now go to the lavatory, wash your face and then back to your class. Everything will be fine." I tried to get out a 'thank you, sister' but just couldn't.

"Oh, Richard," Sister said sweetly as she gave me a big hug The feel of my cheek against the starched white bodice of her uniform was one of the most consoling things I have ever felt. I blubbered, "I loved her!" Sister patted my back saying, "We all did." although I said nothing. I was thinking, *No, not like I did.*

My Mother let me stay home from school the next day.

She said it was because I was running a temperature. But I wasn't. She knew I was just sad.

It was a lifetime later; I was working at the Presidents' Club, a private restaurant for power dining in downtown St. Petersburg on the 20th floor of a building. There were floor-to-ceiling windows with a fantastic view of the shimmering blue Gulf of Mexico. I wore a tuxedo every night.

Once during spring training, the Yankees' owners, coaches and players all came in for dinner. My heart went into my throat when I saw DiMaggio walking in the door. He still looked great with his smooth silver hair, impeccable suit and tie, matching handkerchief. I felt like a little kid again as he walked right past me, his wingtips gleaming.

At this club, we were supposed to respect the guests' privacy and not actually engage them in conversation. But, after dinner when I was pouring coffee, I noticed Joe, off by himself at one end of the table while everybody else talked big business. He seemed a little distant, if you didn't know who he was and what he'd done; you might feel a little sorry for him. I got my nerve up.

"You probably don't remember me, but I met you once before Mr. DiMaggio."

"Did you, son?"

Then I realized how silly that sounded. *Joltin Joe* had likely shaken 100,000 hands. But, I went ahead and told my story about meeting him with Marilyn at the Tides, on the beach.

About halfway through, he seemed to look at me for the first time. I saw him glance at my name tag and then his whole face changed... softened, his dark eyes clouded over and, for a moment, there was the sound of waves and the smell of salt water. It was just like time travel.

I got self-conscious, mumbled some apology for interrupting and backed away.

They had always seemed like the perfect couple to me, Joe and Marilyn. For that brief time, they were America's sweethearts and then, it all came to such a heartbreaking end. Yet, here I was, eking out my humble existence, happily married with a lovely wife and a wonderful son.

Mosquito
by Ray Villadonga

We ride behind mosquito trucks
Inhaling the kerosene and pesticides
On oyster shell dusty roads, we ride our bicycles with pride
Warm summer afternoons, war with water balloons
Kill the man with the ball
Smoking our first cigars
Those were the days, Those hot summer fun ways
When we were so young,
Secret societies,
Climbing the old oak trees

16

We play all day in the sun
Ride to the dump for fun
Fiddler crab astronauts,
Bumble bees your father fought
And greased monkey bars
Those were the days
Those hot summer fun ways
When we were so young
So full of fun

Why I am

Ybor City was a completely different place when I was growing up. It was such a small town. Everybody knew everybody - or else they were related to them somehow. We would catch bass at the pond in Robles Park, we built our own rafts out of bamboo and floated down the Hillsborough River just like Tom and Huck. And, you could pick the fruit right off the trees: oranges, tangerines, grapefruit, mangoes, guavas, Japanese plums. And, people didn't seem to mind... as long as you didn't touch the avocados! They were serious about that; it was kind of a Garden of Eden thing.

I grew up in this idyllic little neighborhood where the houses were well cared for. Most everybody had a nice yard, green lawns of St. Augustine. Most of my aunts, uncles and cousins, as well as my grandparents from both sides of the family, all lived within a few blocks. You could walk anywhere, day or night. Kids played outside until long after the street lights came on.

It was pretty much a porch society in those days with no *AC.*

"Tell your mother, I said hello." Women would say, as I passed. Men sitting back in a porch chair with a big *tabacco* called out the simple greeting, "DiPietra!"

There was a wonderful warmth and vitality with so many of the people sharing a similar background. The Cubans and

17

Sicilian were all from the same few towns. And those from different backgrounds were still from the same working class, hanging on like hell to the status quo with dreams of a better life for their sons and daughters. Christenings, children's birthdays, holiday celebrations, weddings and funerals were all faithfully attended, everyone glad to show their love and support. It was a wonderful time. Between wars, with a chance for all to work or study and plan their future… blissfully unaware of what exactly that future would bring.

Man, you wouldn't believe how incredibly rich that neighborhood was! Walking the brick streets of Ybor was a treat for the eyes and ears, sure but the fragrance of people preparing their favorite food or drink was almost overpowering. Early every morning, the smell of coffee roasting would drift across the city from the south. Then, that whiff of olive oil warming up in a pan to make *huevos fritos*, fried eggs…done till the edges are crisp and brown, to be served over rice or with Cuban toast. Or, could be *platanos* going in the pan…*platanos* go with everything! Ripe and sweet or a little green and salty. And, who could forget the pungent aroma of garlic softening in olive oil, wafting out a window as you walked past? Soon to be joined by onions or peppers or both to make a *sofrito*, the very heart of Latin cooking and the foundation for most of the signature dishes, like yellow rice, black beans, *picadillo*, *ropa vieja*…Old clothes never tasted so good! As well as the *sugo*, the red sauce for pasta. Talk about soul food!

But I gotta tell you, folks; if you don't know already, that, bar none, the most appetizing of all these fantastic cooking smells of Ybor was the Cuban bread. Most everyone loves the smell of fresh bread baking. Imagine going into a bakery anytime and being greeted by that wonderful aroma. And you could get a loaf 3 feet long for what, a couple of bucks? Best money you could ever spend. Ah, that pale crispy crust with the soft white dough inside and graced with the signature palm frond. Nothing else like it in the whole world!

And, of course, the most popular use for the bread is to

make Cuban Sandwiches. You can find Cuban Sandwiches almost anywhere now. I see signs for them all over. Every little gas station, convenience or grocery store, gourmet shop, bar, bakery - I've even had one in Dublin! But did you know that the sandwich that you get here is unlike all the others? You see, if you ask someone from Miami or even Cuba, how to make a Cuban sandwich, they have a whole different method than we do here in Tampa; the difference is subtle but distinctive.

OK, first, you gonna need some Cuban bread! It's the best but in a pinch, any crusty loaf –style bread will do: French, Baguette, Ciabatta. Slice yourself off a piece that fits your individual needs and slit it evenly down the middle. Now, traditionally, the ingredients are layered in a very specific order. First, the ham, marinated and roasted with a lot of cumin for a happy life, covered with a glaze of caramelized sugar and then sliced thin, the thinner the better. I like it so thin you can almost see through it. Then, pieces of tender juicy Cuban pork, bathed in *mojo* for days, a pungent marinade of bitter oranges from Sevilla. Next, the cheese, Swiss,! always Swiss. Imported. From the Alps! A few well-placed dill pickles....not too thick, not too thin. On the top slice, lovingly spread yellow mustard.

Marry the two sides and you're done!

As always, it's a marriage of condiments and cultures, the Spanish ham with the Cuban pork.

This mix for a sandwich goes back to Cuba over 100 years ago and was continued here in Tampa by Cubans interested in preserving their heritage or just to show us what's good! The *difference* being, that here in Ybor, Sicilians made their presence and preferences known. So.... a few slices of Genoa salami...with black peppercorns, were added to make a Cuban sandwich that you will find only in Tampa Bay! I like to think of it as crafted with harmony in mind and in an effort to make everybody happy.

My parents were both born here in the states; my grandparents came over yearning to breathe free, my mom's from Spain and Cuba and my dad's from Sicily. Whenever someone asks me my nationality, I always get a kick out of telling them, "I am a Cuban Sandwich."

SKY KING

Right in the heart of the Ybor, there was a full city block devoted basically to kids. Cuscaden Park was a paradise with open grass fields, basketball courts, baseball diamonds, a full-sized swimming pool and... the Ybor City Boys' Club, my home away from home for all my younger years.

There was something for everyone at the Boys' Club; arts and crafts, wood shop, pool tables, board games. They had a gym and we went on field trips. I went to my first dance there when I was about 10; girls used to ask *you* to dance back then. It was truly another time!

We would make stuff, like lanyards, ashtrays and bookends and it provided our parents with a much-needed break. Yo-yos were the happening thing, so the club would bring in the Yo-Yo Masters - two Filipino brothers who would put on a show: *The Loop the Loop, The Flying Saucer, Walking the Dog, Rock-a-by Baby, The Man on the Flying Trapeze and The Around the World!* Afterwards, they would sell us the newest yo-yos and teach us how to do the tricks.

Sometimes, baseball players would drop by for autographs and some advice. The Cisco Kid and Pancho even showed up in costume and on horseback and cracked us up with their popular, "Ay, Cisco!" "Ay, Pancho."

Joe E. Brown, the comic renowned for his rather large mouth, came to the club and what do you think they gave him? A Cuban sandwich! And Joe E Brown takes this big-ass Cuban sandwich made from an entire long loaf of Cuban bread, opens his big mouth wide and chomps the whole thing in half with one huge bite! All of us kids went crazy when we saw that.

Once, Sky King came to see us kids. His was one of my favorite TV shows. Saturday morning after cartoons and brought to you by Nabisco, I just loved those cookie commercials. He was a modern-day cowboy with a plane, the *Songbird*, as well as a ranch and horses. So, when we found out he was coming to the club and.... that he was bringing Penny, his cute teenage sidekick, I couldn't wait.

Packed into the gym, we went wild cheering when Sky and Penny came in. We listened to their stories, asked questions, laughed at the jokes. Then... it was time to meet them. We all lined up and moved down the row, Penny first and then Sky King.

As I moved along, I noticed that Penny, was looking awfully nice in her cowgirl outfit, white boots with red stars, a soft brown skirt and top, and a little round cowgirl hat that she wore hanging from its cord, laying back on her wavy blonde hair that was shining in the morning light streaming in from the gym's high windows. It was truly the stuff that dreams are made of.

Not only that, she was giving the guys in front of me a little peck on the cheek. This was gonna be great!

Now, I gotta tell you folks, that even though just a kid, I was kind of large for my age, certainly the biggest kid in line. So when I get up to her, she puts her hands on my shoulders, sizes me up with a tilt of her pretty head and shakes my hand!

I couldn't believe it, what a crushing blow! I mean what the heck did I do? Nobody else got a handshake and it's not like I was making kissing noises at her or anything. When she stuck out her hand, I was so insulted that I wanted to knock it away… but, I took it and moved on down the line.

By the time I got to Sky, I was fuming, man. I felt like telling him, "Why don't you get your cowboy outfit in that plane and fly into the blue of the western sky and take your little blonde *bimbette* with you."

Just like all the other cute and popular girls that everybody always wanted to be around, just setting yourself up for heartache and trouble. Forget her!

So, I stomped all the way home, banged through the screen door and headed for my room. My mom was surprised,

"You're home already?"

"Yeah."

"How was Sky King?"

"Great!"

Not fooled, she offered, "Want something to eat?"

"No!"

Oh, my mom knew that couldn't be right. Her concerned face appeared at my doorway, "You feeling alright?"

"Yes!" I whined, wishing for it all to be over. She lovingly felt my forehead, looked into my eyes and in a voice of wisdom asked, "What happened?"

So, I unburdened myself and told her what happened.

"Oh, honey, she just didn't want to lead you on."

"Lead me on? Ma, I'm eight! If she gave me a kiss on the cheek, I was gonna what? Think that she liked me best and we could become boyfriend and girlfriend? Walk around the Boy's Club holding hands? Yeah, she might even take me away with her on the plane, put me into the show! I could be the new character, Richie, the chubby little kid that just moved out west from Florida and keeps falling off his horse! Jeez, Ma, it was just a peck on the cheek! Was that asking too much? It's okay," I asserted, "I'll be fine!"

And I was. In fact, I grew up and found my own cute and popular girl that everybody wants to be around and I married her. Now, every so often, when I'm feeling down, she calls me over, with a sexy little grin, puts her hands on my shoulders, sizes me up, and shakes my hand.

THE MITT

"Hey, Rich! Wanna play? Naw," I answered, "Gotta go." as I trudged across the park towards home.

It wasn't that I didn't want to play. I would've really liked to play. I didn't have to anywhere to go, particularly. I just knew as soon as I told them that I didn't have a glove, the offer would soon be revoked. It's kind of hard to play baseball without one.

I should be used to it: big family, hard-working dad, mouths to feed, not a lot left for trivial things like baseball gloves. No big deal. My mom and dad had been fielding my hints about it for weeks. Christmas was 6 months away, so…what the hell.

"Want something to eat?" My mom welcomes me home with a favorite refrain for her chubby little son. "Sure." is my reply, delivered without much gusto. "How would you like some Cuban toast?" She asks, "Thanks, mom." She always knows just what I need, well almost always, I think, as she serves me the two long pieces of bread slathered with butter.

"It's Wednesday, you know." She throws over her shoulder as she bustles around the kitchen, "your dad's half-day." "Yeah," I say, cheered by the reminder. Maybe he'll have some of those little chocolate milks!

I'm lying in front of the TV watching cartoons when my Dad comes home. He gives my mom a kiss, then they talk in low tones, grownup stuff. I hail him with, "Hey, Pop!" I hear him approach and he stands in the doorway. I feel his eyes on me and I turn giving him a wave. He gives me that

"My Son!" look and chuckle, saying, "You know I had to get a whole new carpet because we could see your imprint in the old one from you lying in front of that TV for 10 hours a day!" With a grin I reply, "Thanks, Dad!" He heads back into the kitchen smiling and shaking his head.

I thought that he was going for his usual after-work nap, when he calls me into the kitchen. With a last look at the TV screen, I amble in. My mom and dad are leaning over by the sink looking at something, whispering. My Dad looks up and sees me then; he swivels around and sticks his hand out saying "How about that!"

He was leaning forward like a first baseman waiting for the throw, and on his big hand was the oldest, strangest baseball glove I'd ever seen! Not only was it beat up and worn, on its last legs but it was split-fingered, something completely foreign to me at the time. The leather was so dark almost black with use and oil. "Whaddya, think, huh? He wants to know with this expectant smile creasing his already creased and sun worn face.

With my mouth hanging open and both my loving parents smiling down at me, I recovered pretty well and gave them the expected, "Is that for me?" "Yes," my mother says and explains that an old friend of my dad's, Red Leto, used to play in a league years ago and he offered it to Pop for me. Dad puts the glove under his arm, yanks it off and hands it over with a "Try it on!" and I did, taking in that wonderful smell of leather. It was pretty big for me, naturally and there were only a few laces left. The fingers on it looked huge! Pounding my fist into it, I noticed there was next to no padding and the web was held together with a single gnarled strand of leather.

But, it was mine and I already loved it. Like all loves, it came with a letdown. The glove was right-handed! And I... was not.

Since I had never had one before, playing bare-handed for years, the problem had never come up. Not wanting to belittle this gift or seem ungrateful, I say nothing about it and go into the backyard to throw a few with my dad.

I slept with the glove that night; I'd rubbed it lovingly with saddle soap, put a ball in it and wrapped my treasure in rubber bands.

Next morning, I was raring to go; my folks said it was all right for me to take my glove with me to school. On the field before class, I experimented with different methods of using the glove, catching with it on my left hand, whipping it off and throwing lefty or wearing it on the right kind of like a first base mitt.

The glove was a little wonky but worked well with that technique and the guys thought it was cool. It was so different from anything they'd ever seen. They kept asking to try it out but I refused, claiming my dad told me not to let anyone else use it. A little white lie but I just couldn't risk it.

I was having so much fun that going in to class was harder than usual but I knew I'd be back out on the field for recess. Ah, *recess*, that wonderful word! Another chance to play but for right now my glove would have to stay in the cubby under the seat of my desk. Even so, I stole glances at it, whenever Sister was at the blackboard with her back turned. Once, she caught me looking down and touching it and gave me hell about it. I was just going to have to be patient. OK, I got it.

The school day was almost done and I was itching to grab my glove and get out there. Sister was at the blackboard and I took advantage to pull out my glove and marvel over it again when I felt a cold breeze and heard Sister's scary voice, "Richard! What did I tell you about that?" Oh no, what a fool I am!

She ripped the glove out of my hands, "Now, I'm going to have to take it away from you. We will give it to the poor children, since you can't be trusted to behave in class."

I was floored. Tears stinging my eyes, I pleaded, "Please, sister! I promise I won't do it again. I won't even bring it to school anymore. I'm sorry." My words fell on deaf ears as she marched to her desk and put my glove in a drawer, slammed it shut and then stood glaring at me. My whole world was crumbling around me! How could this be?

The others in class kept sneaking looks at my tear-stained face, some in sympathy and others completely unmoved by my pain. I spent the rest of the hour in a trance, hoping against hope that Sister would have pity on me at the end of the day and return my glove but she didn't have an ounce of pity. The walk home was interminable, nothing seemed right. Nothing could save me now.

I told my mom that I wasn't feeling well and spent the rest of the day in bed tossing and turning, praying for some form of salvation. I must have fallen asleep because the next I knew my Dad was home and mom was making dinner. I remained holed up in my room wishing it all away. Then, Mom called us to dinner and I crawled out of bed and glumly trudged into the kitchen and took my place at the table.

Doing my best to just get through this, I was almost done when Dad turned to me with a grin and asked, "Did you have fun with the glove today?" I shook my head, tears stinging my eyes. "What's wrong?" my father sensed something. Trying to compose myself, I answered, "Sister took the glove away from me." And, I proceeded to tell him the story.

My father did not look happy, "Didn't I tell you not to play with it in class?" I nodded my head numbly. "Where is it now?" he wanted to know. The worst seemed to be over so I replied, "Sister says she's going to keep it. She's going to give it to the poor kids." My dad dropped his spoon, the sound of it hitting his plate going off like a gunshot. Then, I heard "That Sound" in his voice. Everyone in the family knew the sound all too well and it was a warning signal to all.

"She said that?" he demanded to know. I was so sad and scared all I could manage was a nod. There was a moment of silence and I was hoping it was over when my Dad stood abruptly, knocking his chair back and quietly said, "Get your coat on."

He went into his room and quickly returned with his work jacket on, telling me, "Come on!" "Where are we going, I wanted to know?" Already half-way out the door, he gestured with his arm for me to come and replied, "We're going to talk to Our Lady of Perpetual Help!"   On the trip to the school, my dad seemed to calm down, appearing almost relaxed while a smile played across his lips. Finally, breaking the silence, he told me, "You didn't do anything wrong, son. You're a little boy. Kids want to play; that's what they do. She should know that. I guess she…and he trailed off with a shrug.

The Church was dark but there were lights on in the convent across the street. While the church was beautiful

27

with its stone steps and spires, the convent was a low rectangular brick box surrounded by walls and gates. I'd never seen it at night before. To me, it looked like a prison.

Dad opened one of the iron gates looked around and headed to the back. Along the way, I cautioned him, "Pop, I got to tell you, this Sister Damian, she's pretty mean!" My Dad didn't even break stride but I swear his smile got bigger.

He knocked on the back door; we could see movement in the room through the curtained windows. One of the other Sisters answered and asked us how she could help us. Dad answered that we were here to see Sister Damian and she turned away with a puzzled look, saying, "I'll get her." Through the partially opened door, we could see the nuns setting a long dinner table while the priests sat around drinking wine and smoking.

The table was set with a lace cloth, beautiful silverware and glasses and there were candles flickering in holders that looked like gold.

My grandfather had always been critical of the treatment the poor in Sicily got from the Church. It left him very bitter. He had a favorite refrain that he felt summed it up best, "No money, No Mass."

I was more than a little nervous at the thought of another confrontation with the Sister but my father's big strong arm on my shoulder felt so protective, I began to feel optimistic.

Sister Damian appeared at the door, "Hello, Richard. Yes, Mr. DiPietra, how can I help you?" My Dad was polite as he spoke to the nun, "Sister, I know my son was in the wrong breaking the rules and disobeying but he's a young boy and they can be impulsive as you must know." I gazed up in awe at this man; I thought I knew so well, speaking so calmly and clearly.

Sister replied that she was sorry but Richard has to learn. She seemed to be insulted by the very thought and said she could not return the glove, it was to go into the "Box for the poor as did all confiscated materials.

My Dad's voice had that edge as he answered, "I don't know who these poor kids are supposed to be but I don't think they could be any poorer than me and my family. Not only that, the glove was a gift to my son from an old friend of mine; he knew my son had never had a baseball glove before."

Sister remained unmoved, "Like I said I am sorry but…My father interrupted, "I've been polite. Now, I'm going to tell you. You're going to go get me that glove right now or I am coming in and getting it myself. Now is that clear, Sister? His voice did something with the word "Sister" that left no doubt as to his intentions.

Sister Damian looked a little flustered, finally saying, "I'll see if I can find it." We calmly waited a few minutes on the doorstep, my dad's arm squeezing my shoulder, reassuringly. Finally, Sister reappeared, glove in hand! Intent on having the last word, she said, "Well, I guess we can make an exception this time."

I clutched at my glove, hugging it to my chest and my dad told me to give him a minute. As I moved away, I could hear my dad talking in hushed tones to the Sister, "I don't want to hear that my son was mistreated in any way because of this by you or anyone in the school or the church, do I make myself clear?" Sister Damian suddenly didn't look so tough at all to me. Her voice had lost its edge, "Of course, Mr. DiPietra." My Dad steered me around towards our car and he threw over his shoulder, "Goodnight, Sister."

Walking to the car, I was thrilled to have my precious glove back but as I looked at my Dad behind the wheel on our way home, it occurred to me that I'd had something so much more valuable all along.

Later that year, one of my uncles bought me a brand new glove for my birthday. It was beautiful, a Rawlings fielder's glove, the rich leather a golden brown and best of all, it was a left-hander! I kept my old mitt so my dad and I could have a catch, every now and then.

A few months later, I was playing in a pickup game at Cuscaden Park and after it was over, I noticed a young kid shagging flies with his friends. He was using a paper bag on his hand for a glove. I walked over to watch, noticing that his clothes were a little worn. His pants way too big for him, were cinched up tight with a skinny belt, the end of it dangling down.

As I got closer, I realized he was barefoot, his tough-looking callused feet bristling with sandspurs that didn't even seem to bother him. Under the guise of watching their game, I hung around until I got a chance to approach him and said, "Hey man, I got an old glove I don't use anymore, you want it?" "You kidding, hell yeah!" he responded. "It's pretty old and not in the best shape." I advised him to which he replied, holding up his bagged hand "You see what I got going here?" All right, I said, I'll be back in about 15 minutes."

I took off running across the park with a big smile. Man, he is going to love that mitt!

THE CAUSEWAY

My father would shake me awake at 3:30 in the morning. As a milkman, it was the hour he awoke most every day. He would forego his usual coffee because there would be plenty of that where we were going.

Right next to the big Super Test grounds on Boy Scout Road across from what is now the Tampa Bay Bucs Stadium, there was a small shop squeezed in between the bigger stores around it. This was our first stop. *Chica's Donuts*.

My dad and I were usually the first ones there, tapping on the window until the owner would come out of the back room smiling, to let us in. He was small and slender wearing spotless whites and moving with a pleasant economy. He was *Cubano*, through and through.

31

Dad and the man would quickly dispense with greetings and begin joking in Spanish and talking sports and politics as he went about his opening routine.

A big silver vat took up one side of the shop and he deftly hooked up a hose and began to fill it with oil. He carefully monitored its progress as he moved back and forth between the kitchen and the front. Shaking his head as my dad offered his help between sips of coffee.

Next, he positioned what appeared to be a large funnel suspended from a rack on the ceiling and began to dump bags of flour into it mixing in other ingredients, seeming to do it all by heart without measuring. Then, he added the liquid ingredients, a little at a time, obviously going for the right consistency. By this time, the oil in the vat was beginning to simmer, waves of heat were coming off it and he checked a large thermometer hooked on the side and deemed it ready.

The funnel, looking like an upside-down cannon was swung out over the vat and he began working a trigger mechanism, dispensing perfect rings of dough floating onto the hot oil and quickly filling up the whole vat. It looked like a giant bowl of Cheerios.

Then, he began to carefully tend them. He would circle the vat slowly, holding a large wooden paddle which he used to keep them separate, his sharp eyes flitting from one to the other, gauging when they were ready to be flipped and then scooped out and placed on a wire cooling rack. The golden oil soaked into each one as he finished them simply, with powdered sugar on half of them and cinnamon on the other.

The baker would bring me and my dad a couple as soon as they were ready, watching for our reaction at the delicious first bites and then hustling off to continue tending to the rest of his batch.

This was why I always looked forward to going fishing with my Dad. With a start like that to your day, how could it go wrong? Refreshed, with our bellies full of donuts, we would head on over to the Causeway and try our luck at some fishing.

One Sunday morning, the clouds were low and grey; never a good sign for going outdoors, but my Dad only had one day a week to do something that he liked to do. So, we were up at the crack of dawn, hit the donut shop for our treat and cruised over to the causeway. Dad was particularly happy today because he was going to get a chance to try out his new fishing reel. He had seen it in a small second-hand shop on his milk route and the owner being a long-time friend gave him a good deal. It was a real beauty, a Shakespeare bait caster, well-made and looked almost new with few signs of wear.

The night before, I watched my Dad loading the reel with new line, marveling as the guide slid back and forth distributing the line evenly to avoid snags and backlashes. That morning, he woke me two hours earlier than usual. I could feel his excitement, like a kid on Christmas morning.

Telling the cook about his new toy as we were leaving the shop, his friend joked, "Hope you catch *Un Tiburon*!" My dad smiled in return as he eyed the gathering clouds over the bay.

We parked in our favorite spot near the first bridge with the station wagon safely off the road and climbed down a few feet to the shore. We had a bucket of live shrimp for bait and I put them down in between some rocks where they would be under water and not move around too much.

As usual, with most fishing outings, not much happened. Dad was getting used to his new reel, practicing his cast and return. A few nibbles here and there.
Fishing the bottom, I caught a catfish which my dad took off the hook for me. I was glad because they were scary! Those barbells and stingers could really get you!

Then for hours nothing, except more dark clouds and then the wind started to freshen a bit. Not a lot, but I could sense my dad's concern. Lighting flashed on the horizon, far away. It took a while for the sound of thunder to get to us. I could see him counting the distance in his head. I did the same. It was definitely heading our way. Dad had that look on his face, "Always something!"

He had finally got the hang of the new reel and was enjoying the sheer pleasure of the mechanism, when Bam! Something hit his bait hard. He fumbled for a bit, got it together and struck back twice. Fish on! Whatever was on the other end of his line was not happy and was hauling ass in the direction of Mexico as my Dad wore some skin off his big thumb, pressing down on the reel to make it as tough on the fish as he could.

Then, lightning cracked the sky in half above us! Or, at least that's how it seemed to me! We both ducked instinctively, like that was going to help anything. My dad put his arm out towards me protectively and shouted, "Get in the car, boy!" He didn't have to tell me twice. I ran for the wagon and was completely soaking wet and scared by the time I got there.

There was more thunder, lightning and pelting rain. Through the frosted car windows, I watched my dad standing tall knee-deep in the water playing the fish little by little. Sometimes he gained a little line only to lose it again as the fish doggedly fought for his freedom.

There was another hellatious crack of lightning and my dad bolted for the car, keeping his rod tip up as he sloshed out of the surf and clambered up the rocks to the car.

When he got there, he swung the door open, cranked the window down a bit and stuck his rod into the car as he piled into the wagon. He toweled his face off and grinned at me. And, I realized, he's not scared, he's enjoying this!

Then, he turned his attention back to the reel which had been losing line all that time. With the rod stuck out the window and hell and damnation all around us, my dad continued to pump and reel, sometimes just holding his ground and others reeling like mad to keep up.

Finally, I watched him pause, make up his mind and

hand me the rod saying, "Just hold on to it, boy" As he bolted out the door back into the melee.

He grabbed the line now, tight as a wire and wrapped it around his big fist, taking it in, hand over hand as he worked his way down to the shore. And, then just for a moment, I saw a flash of gold in the wash at the water's edge. Dad lifted it up and headed back to the car.

He swung open the back door and tossed the fish onto the seat. I turned around for a look and saw it was a *rojo!* A big one, its coppery scales glinting in the low light and its tail with two blacks spots on it, like dark eyes looking back at me. Two spots! Probably how this fish got to be so big.

Dad was laughing like a crazy man, part fear, part elation, as he toweled off again. He fired up a cigarette taking two drags and exhaling long plumes of smoke smiling that, "Damn! Did I really just do that!" smile. And, then exclaiming to me, "All right, Rich! We got food for a week!"

When we got home, my dad wrapped the redfish in a towel and took it in to present to my mom, who put her hands to her blushing cheeks, "Ay! Honey, it's so beautiful! How are we going to cook it?"

"I'm gonna cook it Cuban style," he answered with a little twinkle in his eye.

And he did. He cleaned the red and filled the cavity with slices of lemons. Then, he made cuts into the side of the fish and slid slices of lemon in there as well. Chopped onions, peppers and garlic were then spread over the fish and he sprinkled parsley, basil and oregano over it and bathed the whole thing in *mojo* before sliding it into the oven in a casserole dish and telling my mom, "Wake me up in an hour and I'll finish it."

The wonderful aroma of that meal cooking in our oven is still talked about with reverence.

My sisters and even my little brother and I worked together to set the table, sensing that this was not just an ordinary meal. We were all ready and anxious when my dad awoke, drank a quick *café solo* and said with a look at his wife and five children seated around the big kitchen table, "All right, let's eat."

He took the fish out and let it rest while we poured sweet ice tea and took our seats. Then, he reverently coaxed a filet off the fish and slid in onto a plate and continued until only the bones were left, finally, spooning all the juice and vegetables onto each plate until everyone was served. We said grace with heads bowed, feeling truly blessed for the bounty of such a feast.

Everybody in my family is a great cook, including my wife and myself. We learned from the best. Some of us cooked in restaurants, both family style and fine dining and were lucky enough to have eaten at some of the best places around the world.

Yet I can say without a moment's hesitation that never has any meal come anywhere close to that feast, nor will any to come. And, I'm cool with that. Sometimes once is enough, and sometimes... it's even more than that.

GO FLY A KITE

I've always been interested in sports, all of them, watching them on TV that is, but as far as playing the games; football and softball were my favorites. Being on the heavy side, those requiring speed were never going to be my favorite games. So, I stuck with football. Just throwing the ball around was pretty much fun. A football has that beautiful spiral that looks so great in the air and is so satisfying when you watch it right slide into your waiting hands.

It was hard to get enough players for teams. We were usually happy to get 3 on 3 or 4 on 4 but would settle for whatever we could get. My little brother and I spent long hours playing one on one with me on my knees to even it up. Sometimes we'd even soak the playing field, which was our side yard, with water from the hose to give it that black and blue feel. Hobbling into the end zone sloshing through mud could be a hell of a thrill, even on your knees!

Unfortunately, there were not many leagues that played football in Ybor City at that time; mostly softball and Little League. Then, the City of Tampa started an Inter Park league where we would compete with teams from all over the city.

It was flag football, instead of tackle; you wear a rag tucked into your pants and when someone from the other team grabbed it and pulled it, you were considered Tackled or Down. Otherwise, the game was pretty much the same.

Ragan Park put together a pretty good team. We had a couple of good-sized guys up front that jammed up the middle and made it easier for our guys to grab some of the other team's flags. Our quarterback was a baseball pitcher with a great arm for going downfield. We won three games in a row and were feeling pretty proud of ourselves.

Then the kids from Palmetto Beach came to play. They were completely different from any of the other teams we'd played. I swear some of their guys were shaving already. They were big and rough, which intimidated the crap out of us. And that wasn't the worst of it…not by a longshot. They had a team leader like nothing we had seen before. Short and skinny, always with the jokes and wisecracks, you had to love this guy. Until he started playing, that is. The first time he touched the ball, he went all the way down the field without any of our guys laying so much as a hand on him and in his wake half of us were left lying on the ground.

He went on to do the same thing several times in a row. No one seemed to be able to grab the guy's flag! He just slipped away, time after time. Then, as they huddled up, I noticed the other team whispering as they tucked in their star players' flag and I remembered guys at the Boys' Club telling stories about players who would tuck their flag into their pants and then tie it onto their belt loop or even their

37

underwear to make it tough to pull out. I told the guys in the huddle what I suspected and we came up with a simple plan.

With his next snap their guy started with his end around move and everybody on our team shifted sideways putting themselves in position to slow him down and block his path. Surprised, he tried to make up something on the fly and we all converged on him at the same time. One of our older guys grabbed the quarterback and wrapped his flag around his hand pulling at it as hard as he could. There was a big ripping sound as their guy went down and when he got up he had to cover himself because he was holding up what was left of his pants…and there was a big knot tied around his underwear!

You don't get many days like that as a kid, usually, just a lot of disappointment. But that day both sides laughed their asses off. We shook hands and complemented each other, planning on getting together for our next game. And, their quarterback…that smartass, wisecracking little guy. Well, I still see him every so often, weddings and funerals and we have the best time replaying every single moment.

As I said my goodbyes and headed home, I slowed when I noticed a poster on the clubhouse door.
Kite contest at Ragan Park.
Next Saturday, 9 AM Prizes and refreshments.

Hmm, I didn't know how I felt about a contest and prizes but I loved refreshments. Gotta get me a kite!
On the way home, I stopped at my corner store for a Grapette. Tilting it back and letting that sweet cold soda cool me off, I noticed there were a couple of kites wrapped in plastic hanging up for sale. Looking up, admiring the kites, I noticed Joe, the butcher in his white apron smiling at me from the other side of the meat case.

"You like flying a kite? He asked

"Yeah, it's fun, I answered, a little shy. Even though I'd seen him for years behind the counter, we'd never talked before.

"I know how to make beautiful kites," he threw over his shoulder as he worked. "Been making 'em since I was a kid *en Cuba*." He had me. "Is it hard to do?

"Well, you gotta know the trick. Always gotta know the trick. When he turned to me again and saw me looking up at the kites to see if I could discern this so called trick, he added casually, "I can teach you how to make one if you want." I was skeptical. He didn't know me. "Really?"
"Sure", he shrugged. "You're DiPietra, right? You ask your father. If he says OK then we'll do it." I was pretty confident that my dad would be OK with it. He was typical Sicilian, if you needed or wanted something, you made it.
I asked my dad when he got home from work about Joe teaching me and he chuckled, "Sure! Joe's a good butcher. He can damn sure make a kite." I was excited when I went by the store and told Joe it was ok. He thought about it for a minute then said, "Come tomorrow around lunch time."

I showed up early the next day and Joe smiled at me, "You're excited about it already, eh?" I didn't want to admit it but I'd thought about it all night. I couldn't wait for the morning. Checking the clock, Joe took off his apron telling the boss he'd be back soon.

Joe didn't talk much. I guess the job didn't require it. So, we walked in silence to the Cigar box factory on 22nd St. where there were several big drums out on the sidewalk filled with scraps of wood smelling of Spanish cedar. With his practiced eye, Joe pulled out several slender pieces of wood that looked good to him and nodded at me to follow. On the way home, Joe told me a story about Abraham Lincoln being the one who required that all cigars be sold in a box. I thought he was kidding me but who knew?

Turned out to be true!

We made plans to get together the next day. I was happy that it was working out so well and was looking forward to getting to the good part.

That next day, we got down to business. Joe selected the best pieces of wood and helped me cut three all the same size. Then, he stacked them one on top of the other and showed me how to drive a very thin nail right through the very middle of all three pieces. When he turned them over, the sharp point of the nail was sticking up and I carefully hammered it down so it laid flat.

That done, he stood the pieces up and spread them open, two into a big X and the last one straight across the middle. Looking at that simple frame, I could see what my kite might look like!

It was getting late; Joe's wife asked if I'd like to stay for dinner. I said thank you but we always had dinner as a family. His wife smiled and nodded like she understood. Joe explained that my job over the weekend was to cut small grooves in each of the end pieces of wood. "This is where the string will go into all around the frame holding it together." Always the joker, I cracked, "You got it, Boss!" which got a big laugh out of both of them.

Like with most things in life, stringing the kite was a lot easier said than done. Carving a small groove out of an already slim piece of wood was going to take some time. First, I had to get a knife. In our kitchen, my dad kept a drawer full of old stuff that he never uses anymore. Poking around in the drawer I found this old butcher knife. The blade was old and pitted with rust but it looked cool with its curved blade. My dad said I could use it but to be careful because it was sharp.

It was an exacting job but I knocked out the first two with no problem. Then I got sloppy, half way through the third one, I pressed too hard, the blade split the piece of wood and kept on going right into my hand! Hurt like heck and bled like crazy!

My folks were old pros at this; they cleaned it up, stopped the bleeding and put a bandage on my hand. I wish I could say that I took it like a man but I did not. And, worse, my mom overreacted, forbidding me to use the knife anymore. I cried most of the night until my mom came and sweetly told me that my dad would help me from now on with the kite. Finally, the family could get some sleep.

From then on, it all seemed to come together, with my dad helping me every step in the process and my mother promising not to think about it. It turned out to be a pivotal time for me. I can still hear my Dad's voice of reason, "Take your time, son. You best tool is patience. You got all the time in the world." Don't force it. Let the tool do the work, not you." They were lessons that have lasted me a lifetime.

I got the kite strung and took it to Joe for the final step. Over the next week, I worked with Joe on the kite. We used big sheets of tissue paper cut to size, folded over the strings and glued together. It was starting to look like a kite. Joe told me to leave the kite with him, he had something to do with it and I said my goodbyes feeling proud of myself.

Next time that I went by the store, Joe said he had something to show me and I should visit. When I arrived, Joe and his wife were in high spirits and seemed happy. He went into that back room and came out with the kite that he had finished. I was flabbergasted. The kite was in the shape of a hexagon, which alone made it look so different than any other. Joe had used bright stripes of blue and red and a single white star near the top to set it all off.

"Whaddya think?" He asked offering it up. Looks great was all I could think of. Do you know what this is? He wanted to know.

It took me a minute. "a flag?"

"You are sharp! Yes, this is *La Estrella Solitaria,* the Cuban flag, which prompted me to add, "I thought it looked familiar."

Overhearing us, his wife comes in from the kitchen, "*Pero, José,* you have to tell him the story! It is such a good, story!" She proceeded to tell the story of a young man, a Cuban freedom fighter who went to New York City to get money for the revolution. He had a very hard time being away from home and began to think of giving up. Once, after a long hard day with no success, he rested on a park bench, fell asleep and dreamed that a flag was flying over Cuba.

When he woke and opened his eyes, the colors of the sunset were so beautiful; it seemed to blend into his dream of a flag for Cuba. Excited, he told his wife of the dream and she offered, "I will sew it for you."

There were blue stripes for the ocean, white stripes for the purity of their dreams of a free Cuba and the lone white star on a red triangle for the blood spilled by the heroes of the revolution. I was impressed with the story. I don't think I had ever been so impressed before. I felt so proud.

A few weeks later, I showed up at the trailer asking for Joe. His wife was pleasantly sweet as usual. "Would you like to come in?"

"I just wanted to tell Joe that I won the highest flying kite and the best kite overall!" Beaming, she exclaimed, "How wonderful! I'll have to tell Joe, he'll be so happy."

There was an awkward moment and I thought she might need to get back to her cooking or something, so I turned to leave. She stopped me to say, "You know, we never had any children of our ow but this time, Joe working with you, it's been good for him. He's worked hard all his life, all he's ever done is work. But, whenever you two get together, he always sings your praises! I'd never heard the phrase before. It took me a while but I thought about it as I walked, and about halfway home, I started to feel pretty good.

I've made so many things throughout my life. I worked in wood, like my dad taught me—tables, chairs, bookcases, even boats. But sadly, I never made another kite. The box factory closed and there just wasn't anywhere that I could get the thin strips of wood. But, I still know how to make one. I see kites for sale but none of them would hold a candle to my *Estrella Solitaria*. I guess thrilling to the sight of something you fabricated by hand rising on the wind and then dancing on the end of your string is largely a young man's game. I'd be more than willing to share my knowledge with any interested kite fliers out there. Sure would like to make at least one more though. Pass the torch. Or kite.

BIRRA

My dad never drank beer. He would drink red wine, once in a while, homemade like my grandfather used to make. My grandfather brought his family over from Sicily in the 20's and settled in Ybor City in a nice little neighborhood lined with brick streets.

Nonno was always making and fixing things. That was pretty much his job. He had a little shed in the back where he would fix bicycles, repair shoes or do woodwork. And he also used to make wine, just a little for the table and friends or family. They were big jugs of dark red wine.

But when he got here, he figured maybe, I'll start making beer, "*Americane* love beer, no? *Birra e buona!*" And, as for Prohibition? "Bah, just for my family who gonna know?"

So, he set himself up with a couple of wine barrels that he had and, according to my dad, made the beer in the Sicilian-style.

You bake some bread with a lot of yeast in it and then break it up in the water, add some sugar, probably a lot of sugar, too. Sicilians love everything sweet. Put in some dried fruit: dates, raisins, apricots; add some herbs: basil and parsley, for sure. Cinnamon, cloves; you heat it up and just wait to drink it.

At this time, my dad was just a kid working at the Ferlita Macaroni factory in Ybor City on 22nd St. He was already a supervisor of a small group of younger kids that helped out and ran errands and deliveries.

One day, his younger sister came rushing up the stairs to the factory, calling for my dad, "Dominic! We need you at the house in a hurry. Papa needs you real bad!"

My father told his boss and then took off running for their house just a few blocks away. Flying down the sidewalks and alleyways, cutting through yards with his mind racing, my father worried about his father. "What could it be?" he wondered, "A fire?"

He had to detour around the scary dogs that would always chase him. And, he couldn't go straight down his street to El Reloj, the cigar factory because there had been an armed robbery last week and he heard there was still blood on the sidewalk. So, no way he was going to go by there!

He was getting close now.

He didn't smell any smoke. He did smell something though; he just had no idea what it was. Turning the final corner to his block, that S*omething* stopped him right in his tracks.

Because S*omething* had happened with the beer.

Maybe, it blew a bung or it overflowed - whatever.

Something in the brewing process had gone terribly wrong and now, beer and foam were spewing out of the doors and windows of the shed and flowing like a river down the driveway, then turning like a tributary and running into the street and down the gutters!

The whole family was out there doing their level best to staunch the flow and clean up everything they could, using pots and pans, mops, towels, blankets, buckets, anything they could find; desperate to remove all trace of the beer before it drew the attention of someone in authority. The smell of the beer was everywhere and the foam was knee high on the brick streets!

My grandfather was the general leading the charge, organizing the effort, marshalling the troops, trudging through deep beer foam with a snow shovel and loading up one wheelbarrow after another as quickly as he could muster. He didn't know what the penalty was for making beer - but it couldn't be good and he damn sure did not want to go back to Sicily!

The girls were smarter; they were using sheets like you would a big fish net, with one of them on each side scooping up foam and dragging it to the back of the house out of sight.

Nonna, my grandmother, had a hose out and she was spraying off everybody one at a time, as fast as she could and then toweling them off. But, unfortunately, nothing much could be done about the smell!

Well, the family finally got it all cleaned up and afterwards, sat around the kitchen table, relieved and laughing themselves silly while Nonno swore non-stop in Sicilian. Italian is such a great language to cuss in and Sicilian is even better. As my grandfather finally calmed down, he also swore that from now on he would make only wine, *"Minga Birra!"*

My dad lived a nice long life filled with food, family and fun and during that time, I never once saw him drink a beer. Curious, I asked him once, why he didn't. A soft smile came to his face and then he told me this story.

JAIBA!

Every afternoon at Our Lady of Perpetual Help for lunch time, the bell would ring and we'd all bolt for the door, flooding the streets and sidewalks, reveling in the freedom to roam, to play, to eat and drink, because that's what kids do.

Some would head for the ball field or basketball court and some even to the church. The wonderful sound of children playing would fill the air.

Yet, many kids could be seen milling on the far corner of the school grounds outside the gates and I was invariably among them, waiting. We were anxiously expecting our favorite thing and the best part…it was going to be delivered to us.

As we crowded together, looking both ways, up the street and down because you could never be sure where it would come from, suddenly we would hear that distinctive call, "Jaiba! Jaiba!" This would fuel our excitement and hunger. Then, when he was sighted coming 'round the corner, we all went nuts. For the man was here!

He was known as the Devil Crab Man to generations of Tampeños. He and his wife had hand-made thousands of some of the best street food that you would ever want to eat: The Devil Crab. With our few coins in hand, we queued up to wait our turn and our shot at the best snack ever.

He would always be by around lunch time, a typical *Cubano* - quick-witted and smart-assed but friendly as hell. We usually waited quietly with our eyes on the prize – a Miranda devil crab. We chatted as we moved along until finally, it was your turn.

You paid your nickel; that's right these delicious treats would only cost you a nickel! The devil crab was nestled in wax paper that was twisted on the ends to keep it safe until it reached your mouth. He would use the bottle of hot sauce deftly, plunging it into the filling and revealing all of its delicious goodness. As he loaded the devil crab, He would always ask how spicy you wanted it. *"Con Picante o Sin Picante?"*

Although I firmly believe that he gave everybody the same amount of hot sauce. Once when I complained to my father about Miranda giving us too much, the old man chuckled in reply, "You don't know what's good, boy!"

This simple delicious treat didn't appear by itself! The whole Miranda family contributed in one way or another. Early every morning the father would be at the docks to buy the fresh blue crabs. Meanwhile, the family would have the *sofrito,* peppers, onions and spices cooking on the stove since the night before.

If you've ever cleaned and cooked crabs, you know what a labor of love it is. The shells are sharp and tough to get open, and the yield is not much but it's such a delicacy. Once the crabmeat is harvested, it has to be picked through meticulously to remove all the little pieces of shells, for biting into a shell would ruin it for many customers.

The Mirandas usually got loaves of Cuban bread delivered every day, like we all did, slapped onto nails on their front porch. One loaf was fresh and one was day-old. The fresh loaf was for the filling and the day-old grated into crumbs for the delicious crispy, crunchy coating.

It was a family affair to assemble all the devil crabs and when they were ready, the Dad took to the streets. He would cruise by all his favorite places, hawking his wares, the shipyard, the can companies and cigar factories. Sometimes he made several trips a day going home for more crabs to sell and heading back out.

When I first knew him, he rode on a bicycle with a basket on the handlebars for the crabs. Then as the demand for the devil crabs grew, he got a scooter with a warming tray to keep his treasures hot. And, then he upgraded to an old ice cream truck converted to keep things hot rather than cold.

Again and again, Miranda proved himself and his family to be incredibly resourceful and hard working. The work and the long hours put into it was something only a whole family could maintain.

Because of the hard work, the Mirandas were able to flourish during the difficult years, including two wars and all the changes affecting the working class of Tampa, which was an awe-inspiring feat for immigrants of that time. And, the whole family benefitted.

The Mirandas were able to help their children to get a good education and become successful in their chosen professions, and along the way they inspired generations of hardworking Tampeños to follow their bliss and discover ways to provide something new and appealing for those to follow.

Alll because they could provide something that people would desire and talk about, even to this very day. And, they accomplished this something out of their own initiative and hard work. Especially, something so sweet!

Or should I say, So *Picante*!

NOCHE BUENA

Growing up in Ybor City *Noche Buena,* the celebration of Christmas Eve was the highlight of the year. My Aunt Nena's house on Holmes Avenue, a small street just off La Avenida de Republica de Cuba was always the site of the party.

There were 11 aunts and uncles in my mother's family. Along with their husbands and wives, children and friends, you could expect 50 or 60 people in and out through the night. Especially, since almost everyone lived within a few blocks in those days. The children would share their expectations of presents and compare how much they had grown. Older cousins might have a new boyfriend or girlfriend to introduce to the family, usually being led around with that dazed look in their eyes, overwhelmed by the din and the sheer number of greetings.

As usual in any family, it was all about the food. A big ham smelling sweet with caramelized sugar; lechon, a roast pork, tender and juicy with mojo, yellow rice and chicken; black beans and loaves and loaves of Cuban bread.

And, of course, there were deserts: homemade flan, pies, cakes, brownies, cookies and pastries from the bakery. A true feast worthy of such a large, loving family.

A long table would be set in the dining room with the smaller children's tables in the living room.

Even so, there was no way that everyone could sit down and eat at the same time. So, it was done in shifts, very informally, with the moms alerting their broods when the time was right.

The family was also too large for exchanging presents but we did have our own Santa! My mom's brother, Mariano had moved up to Virginia years ago and always sent a huge box of gifts for the kids, to be opened on Christmas Eve.

There were simple things like pajamas, flannel shirts and slippers but we anxiously looked forward to it all year. We would show each other what we got, trying on clothes. The sweetness of youth.

Afterward, as the women began to clean up, the men would head for the back room to drink, smoke and play poker. I could not resist being drawn to this traditional gathering. Each man had his cigars or cigarettes; everybody smoked back then and each with their glass of whiskey or beer.

The talk was often loud, sometimes a little coarse, but always funny with jokes in Spanish, stories of co-workers and gossip about movie stars, boxers or ball players. And, all of it punctuated by the patter of the card game, "Eight to the pair of jacks – no help. Ten to the king/queen, possible straight!" It was like listening in on a secret meeting.

One night, as I stood next to my dad, looking over his shoulder, someone needed help from the next room. With a look at his cards and then at me, he said, "Finish playing the hand for me, son. Nothing fancy, now; just call, don't raise." And, he was gone. Sliding into his warm seat, I looked around at a table full of men I'd known my whole life but who, suddenly, didn't seem the same, at all. I felt like I was walking into the lion's den.

My uncle, Aniceto, the patriarch, sat at the head of the table. He was the only one in the family that had been born in Spain. He was quite old; his face was like a mask. Aniceto was Basque, spoke very little English, so almost everything he said was completely unintelligible to me but he enjoyed playing the game, drinking shot after shot of whisky.

Next to him sat Raul, a big, florid character, dark as a crow, with a prominent belly that was hard like a rock. He was always challenging the kids to punch him in the gut as hard as they could which only made him roar with laughter. He liked to expound to us about his philosophy of gambling, "Pá lante y pá lante, if I lose ten dollars, next time, I bet twenty. If I lose twenty, next time I bet fifty!" It seemed like an absurd idea to me, but he was often the big winner.

Then came three brothers in a row: Bebe was a mild sweetheart of a guy who said little, played cautiously and enjoyed the camaraderie. Sitting next to him was his brother, Perfecto, who everybody called, Johnny. He had a little twinkle in his eye and loved to regale the table with stories he had heard of celebrities, especially bullfighters of whom he was most fond. Johnny was a stubborn player, chain smoking throughout, his fingers stained from the unfiltered cigarettes that he favored.

Then, there was Titin, easy-going, quiet, whose wife, Margaret would make several trips to the back room to see how things were going, meaning how much her husband might be winning…or losing.

Next, were two of my favorite uncles, Paco and Manuel. They were similar in looks and age, dark haired and handsome; I thought they were the coolest. Paco, with a dark lock of hair always falling across his forehead, a cigarette clamped between his teeth, squinting to keep the smoke out of his eyes and Manuel, the storyteller, entertaining the table with the latest jokes, playing all of the parts with every eye on him until the explosion of laughter with the punch line, always in Spanish and a little risqué, I imagined.

51

The cards were dealt out one at a time with bets in between each round, some raises causing others to fold their cards, "Too rich for me." I kept cautiously throwing in my chips, "I call." My voice sounded ridiculously tiny among that company.

Little by little, it ended up with me and one of my uncles left playing. I had two pair, fives showing and threes as my hole cards; just an OK hand, while my uncle had two Big Scary Kings staring at me. He raised, I called. He raised again, not at all the kindly uncle figure that I knew or thought I knew. I heard somebody say, "Coño, Johnny! Suelta el niño. My uncle's eyes never left mine as a thin smile played across his lips and he answered, "He knows what he's doing." As my little hand hesitated over the chips, one of my older cousins leaned in and advised me, "He's gonna make you pay to see his cards, Rich." And then he encouraged me with a nod and a smile. I heard my voice shaking as I said, "I call." "All right," my uncle smiled across the table, "What you got?" "What you got?" I shot back, "I'm the one that called!" This brought a roar of laughter from the men, while my uncle just shook his head, chuckling and said with a shrug of his shoulders, "You're lookin' at it," gesturing to his two kings. I turned over my hole cards and everyone laughed again when they saw the two pair!

I was raking in the pot which looked like a king's ransom to me, as my dad returned and asked, "What happened?" The men all responded at the same time, "Richard won! The kid outlasted Johnnie! Won with two pair!" My dad was beaming, "That's the way we do it, son!"

In a daze, I headed back to the front of the house feeling…I don't know…taller. Later that night, we drove home with my mom and dad cuddling for warmth in the front while my sisters chatted in the back seat. I was sprawled lying down in the back of the station wagon with my little brother by my side.

As we slowly wended our way through the brick streets of Ybor, stars were brightly shining out of a dark blue

Christmas sky.

RAIN

He didn't do anything wrong, that cop, on that night. It wasn't his fault that he appeared on our front porch in the middle of the night looking stricken in his uniform. He changed our lives with a single question. "Is this the residence of Cynthia DiPietra?"

And, nothing and I do mean *nothing*, was ever the same again. An evening I would spend the rest of my life trying to forget with images and sounds that have lasted a lifetime.

On that night, I remember, as he was leaving, I looked up and said, "Thank you, Officer." He nodded and hurried down our front steps into his waiting car. I watched him for a moment as he took off his hat and placed it on the seat next to him. He ran his fingers through his hair then banged the steering wheel hard with his fist before starting up and cruising slowly down the dark street. Not wanting to face the night ahead, I took my time closing the door, little by little.

For us, before that night were all those golden days. Days spent at Pass A Grille beach with the whole family, wonderful occasions at the causeway or huge gatherings for *Nochebuena*. Even the simple pleasure of eating together as a family at the big table in the kitchen would no longer be the same. We were still a family I know, just diminished in number so to speak. But, I think of that cop often, his life after that night, and wish him well. That night must have been hell for him as well.

It is hours later when the officer returns home. He hangs up his uniform in the closet, takes a long hot shower and goes into the kitchen and kisses his wife. She sees immediately that he is upset. He tries to tell her about his evening but becomes so emotional that he can't finish. "Oh, Sweetheart," she says and holds him close.
"I don't think I can do this anymore," he finally says.
"I want to be a teacher, not an enforcer. I think I would be a good teacher."

"Darling," she answers, "You would be so good at that!" Relieved, he holds his wife close for a long time.

Giving her a kiss, he asks, "How's the boss?"

"Great," she smiles and sighs, "Haven't heard a peep all night."

"Well," he grins and reaches for her hand, "let's take a look at this little fella!"

They pad down the hallway quietly and turn in at the next room. The lights are low and there is a mobile of sea creatures dangling over the crib. A small baby is on his back, stretched out in his pajamas, one arm over his head with his tiny fist clenched. He looks like a superhero in miniature, ready to zoom into the sky. They stand shoulder to shoulder, smiling down and then back at each other.

GASPARILLA

Your name can make you who you are. The name you are born with can affect your personality, your future, your happiness. What then, with a nickname - born in a moment of humor, often at your expense but then lovingly tended, repeated by friends, loved ones... till it becomes a modifying force in how others look at and feel about you, both, upon first meeting you and hearing the name and over time as they grow comfortable and intimate with using it. How else to explain that mature, accomplished, respected people still answer to a nickname from their youth and most of the time, cheerfully.

And, in Ybor City, we had the names.
Papo, Papi, Pepe,
Chupe, Kiki, Pico,
Tico, Chiqui,
Chico, Chichi... Tata,
Mono, Moquito, Titin,
Chino, China,
Nena, Nene,
Nino, Tino,
Moco Brain!

I also knew a *Chocolaté*, a *Coco*, and a *Bardahl. Chupi*...Wait, did I say *Chupi* already? That's ok, he was a great guy. I even knew a guy named Guppy, what is up with that?

My all-time favorite though was *Bacalao*, which is a fish...a cod. Why he was called this, I have no idea but his was the first nickname that I remember, over 50 years ago at the Boys' Club.

Being that it was Ybor City, I bet you thought the names would all be like: *Big Tony… Little Tony… Baby Tony… Frankie Fish… Two Bits.* Like that, right?

Yeah, we had those guys, the real deal, not like the ones in movies or on TV. But, by then, most of the old timers were gone, in one way or another. And with them went the old ways. Younger men were now walking the line, usually into the more victimless crimes. I grew up with them, uncles…cousins…friends. Men with a deep-rooted distrust of authority and a strong desire to control their own lives. They preferred to rely instead on what really mattered to them: good food, laughter and the love of family. To me, they were just men… with nice homes, who dressed well, ate well and lived well. Nobody laughed like these guys!

Right about now, I bet you're thinking…boy are you sugar coating it! A little naïve, aren't we, Richard? Well, back then, you might've been right but now with a much older heart, it just doesn't seem so clear.

It was February 1967 and the *Gasparilla* children's parade. I'm cruising the streets with my teenage buddies, when one of my uncles sees us and calls me over. "Hey, Rich, do me a favor. You and the guys lean against this fence, here. There was this *bobbo*, who was yellin' at the kids for leaning on it. Made 'em cry. Let see what he does with big people, eh?" Over my uncle's shoulder, I could see a few of my younger cousins standing near the street. They looked shook up; one of them was even wiping her tears as she gave me a little wave.

So, my buddies and I all lean against this white picket fence. It wasn't long before we hear the slap of a screen door and look back to see this mean-faced guy striding towards us with this big stick in his hands. He starts whacking the back of the fence with the stick and yelling at us, "Get off the fence! I don't want you leaning on my fence. I already told them that."

At this, my uncle whirls around to confront the guy,

"This, your fence?" I was surprised my uncle's voice was so nice and easy.

"Yeah," the guy says. "This, your house?" my uncle counters.

"Yeah." the guy answers, kind of stunned at the sudden change in the atmosphere.

My uncle sets him up, "What... you rent?"
Now, the guy's not sure what's going on, "No...I." Taking his time, my uncle asks, "Show me some proof, this is your house, this is your fence." Trying to get back his edge, the guy reaffirms, "It's mine!"

Looking around, innocently, my uncle replies, "I don't see nothin' here... you got something in writin'?"
"What?" the guy's baffled. My uncle pounces, "Show me some proof...you got proof? A deed with your name on it, a survey that shows this fence is part of your property? *Something.* You just can't go around scaring people away without some *proof!*"

The man stood frozen with doubt in his eyes and his mouth hanging open. Then he hurries away. Trying to save face, he shouts through the screen door, "I'm gonna call the police!" I shoot a worried look at my uncle who just turns to me with a big laugh, "Good luck with that, eh, Rich?" Then, he leans back against the fence with his arms crossed and calls out, "All right, kids. You can come on back and lean against the fence now and watch the parade. The man said it was... *okay.*"

Say what you will about the stereotypical, sensationalized versions of these men but who among us would not love to have someone help and protect them; right the petty wrongs; side with them, automatically, against anybody even the *Law,* just because they're family.
Grease the wheels, put in a good word, cut through the red tape...and all done with style and humor and out of a love for family. Go on; give me your best argument.

WEST TAMPA
Ray Villadonga

Put on your shoes. Put on your dress, my Signorina.
To Cacciatore's we will go this sunny day. *Gabagool,* Italian
sausage, palomilla. Mortadella, bottle of rosé. Let's go out
and get a cup of Cuban coffee. *El gallo de oro.*They fry and
scramble eggs! West Tampa Sandwich shop, it calls me like a
siren *Caldo gallego* and old men with bad toupees.

THE CIRCUS

My mother spoke Spanish beautifully, my father
spoke Spanish and Italian. When I asked my dad where he
learned Spanish, he said, "In school," like he'd taken classes

or something, and when I asked, "What school?" he grinned and replied, "V. M. Ybor." That was his grade school when he first came to Tampa.

You see, my dad, like so many of the Italians learned his Spanish in the school yard. It's the kind of little Tampa joke that my dad just loved. In our house my parents used Spanish like a secret language so we kid would not understand. They spoke to us only in English and that's how we spoke to each other.

So as Latin as I looked, I never learned. There were relatives and friends of mine who didn't seem to have any problem with it, rattling off to each other or someone on the street. But me, I just learned the basics... cuss words, ordering food and descriptions of female anatomy.

As a boy I would sit at the foot of the table and listen to my father and my uncles talking and joking in Spanish and I would laugh when they laughed, as if I understood. This would really crack them up and even at that age I was a clown for a good audience, so I kept it up. I faked it so well that now, 60 years later, I have to ask people talking to me in Spanish, "*Lentamente, por favor*" Go slowly.

Oh, there were some embarrassing moments when someone finally realized that I had no proficiency beyond what a five-year-old could muster but nothing too traumatic, until I went to the circus.

Ah, the circus! What a day when Barnum & Baileys came to town! The elephants and the lions, the clowns and the acrobats and my personal favorite, the high wire act.

I must have seen the movie, *Trapeze*, at the Tampa Theatre about 5 or 6 times and sure; it was largely to get another look at Gina Lollobrigida in that circus outfit. But, I also envied Burt Lancaster and Tony Curtis looking so sleek and muscular in those white tights. And to be that athletic, man! I particularly loved the white tape around their wrists. I remember after the movie walking around with adhesive tape on my wrists for weeks with everyone, especially my mom asking, "Are you okay, did you hurt yourself?"

Florida has always been a big circus state. Ringling has its home here after all, and there is even a clown school in Sarasota. Then in the 70's near Orlando, someone opened Circus World, a chance to experience circus life firsthand. Obviously, this was before liability suits became so popular.

Here, you could have your heart's desire; if that was to dress up like a clown and jump out of a little car with 20 other clowns; ride a horse bareback, juggle, tumble or, that's right… swing on the flying trapeze.

They had all the training aids in place to help you with the more difficult acts, like for the trapeze, a safety net, of course, as well as a harness with a rope to let you down easy. Seemed like a dream come true.

Luckily for me, I had a buddy, Manuel, from the old neighborhood that was into it, too. We talked about it for a few weeks and finally got up our nerve and headed east… to the circus. Now, Manuel was from a Latin family, too but both his parents were Spanish. His circus hero was Gilbert Roland, dark and handsome with that pencil-thin moustache and that cool accent. Mine was Burt Lancaster and I drove my buddy crazy on the drive over working on my Burt impersonation, "Tonight, we're goin' for the triple!"

So we get there, nervous but excited and we walk into the tent and see the net and the swings way the hell up in the air…we about shit a brick. Then, we meet our trapeze coach and the guy looks just like Gilbert Roland, leotards, white tape on his wrists and all!

We introduce ourselves and tell him we're from Tampa, he beams, "*¿Habla español?*"

Manuel and I look at each other and then smile and nod, "*Si, Señor!*" We want Gilbert Roland to like us after all.

So, we joke around in kitchen Spanish for a while until he gets down to business, telling us how to secure the harness around our waist, deal with the safety rope and climb the narrow ladder to the platform about 30 feet up in the air.

Speaking mostly in Spanish, he's very casual about it

like it's no sweat and he seems to be enjoying us.

Manuel and I keep looking at each other, checking to see if we're getting it but I wasn't getting a damn thing. It was all so fast!

My friend kept nodding at me in a way that reassured me that he would fill me in when we got to the top.

The rope ladder took some getting used to but half-way up, we were swaggering like old pros and I was doing my best "Burt Lancaster." As we step onto the platform and see that swing tethered to one of the ropes, it starts to hit us this is as real as we ever imagined, we started cracking jokes just to mask our fear.

We see Gilbert Roland dance up the ladder, dust his hands, grab his trapeze and fly out into space like a bird. He lands gracefully on the stand on the opposite side of the tent and the shouts over to us, "*Vamos!*"

Manuel and I look at each like two of the Three Stooges. We each take a harness hanging from a rope and start to fumble with the straps. And then, my friend asks a question that sends a chill right up my spine, "What did he say about putting on the harness?"

Turning to him in shock, I ask "Whaddya mean what did he say, didn't you get that part?"
"I couldn't understand a damn thing," he said.
"I thought you had the good Spanish."
"He said something about rope."
"Oh, you're a big help!"

Trying to save some face but up against it now, we start dredging up all the scraps of the language we can think of and yelling them across the empty space to the man on the flying trapeze. *Señor, no sabe*...uhh...I began
No sey, It's no sey!, Manuel corrected me.
OK, I tried again. *Senor, no entiende*....
No! No entiendo!, Manuel corrects me in frustration
"What...you're giving me tenses now!"

61

Meanwhile, Gilbert Roland is clapping his hands together and encouraging us with a "Hup!" as he swings back and forth, rattling off in his rapid fire Spanish, "*Ven pa'ca!*" Desperate, I gave it another shot, *"Lo siento, señor...pero, no entiendo que...que..."* Manuel jumps in to help, *"Que tu dices, tell him que tu dices!"*

Gilbert encouraged us with a "Hup! *Coge la barra suave.*"

In frustration, I lash out at Manuel, "Again with the Hup! Hey, I'm doing the best I can here, Señor Latino guy."

"Why don't you give him your Burt Lancaster?" my wise-ass buddy says. "Et tu, Manuel, et tu?"

"Que pasa?" Gilbert can't take it anymore, he starts working his way down and over to us. This scares the crap out of me, "Oh, man, the guy's coming over here! What the hell we gonna do? *Que pena!* Do you know what that means?"

"Yeah, I know what *Que pena* means," my buddy snaps. "Do you know what, *Vete pa carajo* means?"

We see Gilbert shaking his head. As he reaches our platform, we start fumbling with the language again and he stops us and says in perfect English, "Why the hell didn't you tell me, *come mierdas!*"

Well, that cracked us up and broke the ice. He quickly explained the basics to us, asked with a dashing smile if we "Got it?" and then was off to his place on the swing. "Put your hands closer together...*mas cerca.* Swing out, *afuera!* Hup! All of a sudden... I'm the man on the flying trapeze! "Go higher, *al cielo,*" he explains, "I'll tell you when to let go. Ready? Hup!"

And I flew right into his arms, well, his hands. I was glad that I had my wrists taped! Gilbert swung me back and then on the way out gently let me go and the guys on the ropes lowered me into the net. Holy JC, what a thrill!

Manuel went next and then we both went again. Afterwards, Gilbert and the other guys were all chuckling over us as we said thanks and goodbye, but Manuel and I couldn't have cared less. We had done it!

I learned my lesson that day... and a way to

communicate my limited understanding of the language. Whenever I meet someone who speaks Spanish and after a few words of introduction, they ask, "Habla Español?"

I always answer, *Tengo seis o siete palabras, y no mas.*

I got 6 or 7 words and that's about it!

UN MOMENTO

Spanish Translation by José Suarez

Los padres de mi mamá vinieron de Cuba ya hacía años, cuando aún había muy buenas relaciones entre los dos países. A los americanos les gustaba todo lo que venía de Cuba: la comida, la música, los bailes y, sí, hasta la gente. Mi abuela vivió, en una casita de Ybor City, hasta la edad de noventa y pico años. Crio a diez hijos y nunca aprendió a hablar inglés; mejor dicho, nunca *tuvo* que hablar inglés. En la bodega de la esquina, en el hospital, en la panadería, en la farmacia, todos hablaban su lengua. Nos hablaba a nosotros, sus nietos, en español y, aunque yo no lo hablaba muy bien, ella y yo hacíamos el esfuerzo por comunicarnos lo que es esencial del amor y la vida.

Siempre me molestó que nunca dominé el español. Mamá lo habla requetebién; ¡Papá hablaba español e italiano! Yo, sin embargo, sólo sabía lo básico—las malas palabras, el vocabulario mínimo para poder pedir en los restaurantes latinos y, desde luego, las partes pudendas de la anatomía femenina.

Siempre soñé con que el idioma me surgiera, por arte de magia, todo claro y disponible y que al menos pudiera sostener una verdadera conversación en una de las lenguas maternas de mis antepasados. Sin embargo, más adelante, se me cumplió el sueño gracias a mi abuelita cubana.

Anduve fuera por unos años y, por consiguiente, dejé de ver a mi abuela. Sus hijos eran ya mayores y vivían aparte cuando regresé. Ella, una ancianita dulce y generosa, insistía en vivir sola en un barrio que había decaído con los años.

Al regresar al barrio, me detuve en la *La Segunda Central* para comprar una flauta de pan cubano. Después de pasar el Parque Cuscaden, más allá del depósito de agua y del hospital, en la esquina al frente de la bodega Shirley Ann's, llegué a la casita de madera de mi abuela. Toqué levemente en la puerta metálica a la espera de su calurosa bienvenida a mi inesperada visita. ¿Abuela? Ni un sonido. Al mirar por la tela metálica, vi que estaba de pie en el medio de la sala. Ya un poco preocupado, me dejé entrar y me le acerqué diciéndole "Abuela".

Abuelita siempre había sido bien bajita (ni siquiera medía 5 pies) y el cabello, antes negro como el azabache, ahora se le veía veteado por numerosas canas. Casi siempre se lo recogía en una trenza que dejaba caer por la espalda o hacía de ella un moño. Ahora, lo tenía suelto y esparcido, así como un abanico grande que le daba hasta los pies. Rodeada de motas de polvo que resplandecían a la luz del sol, parecía una santa de estampa. Aun así, ni se movía ni chistaba. Hola, abuela. ¿Cómo estás? ¿Todo bien? Nada. Algo sucedía. Ni cuenta se daba de que yo estaba presente. Intenté otra vez.¿Abuelita, estás bien? Por fin, al ella contestarme en su melifluo español, logré entender con dificultad.

Tengo 93 años de edad . . . hace 15 días . . . ¡tenía 23! Paseábamos por el Malecón y las olas estaban tan altas que tratamos de echarnos a correr, mis amigos y yo, pero el agua

nos empapó. Nos mojamos tanto . . . el pelo . . . todo el vestido . . . el mío estaba cubierto de camelias . . . íbamos a . .
. .

En ese momento, titubeó. Un poco desorientada y, a la vez, un poco triste. No recuerdo haberla visto triste nunca. Le sonreí a esa su cara tan conocida, a esos ojos claros tan azules como el mar distante que llevaba por dentro. Entonces, poco a poco, ella fue alzando la manita hasta tocarme en la mejilla y respondió, Sí, muy bien.

Ya recompuesto, le di un fuerte abrazo. La sentía tan frágil. La conduje al sofá donde nos sentamos por largo rato, de manos dadas, intercambiando sonrisas, haciéndonos preguntas sencillas. Las palabras me surgían como una memoria, como si siempre las hubiera sabido, pero que no podía pronunciarlas sino hasta ahora, a una edad adulta.
Por fin llegó la hora y me le despedí con un beso en la cara. Abuelita me siguió hasta el viejo y crujiente portal. Se había puesto una bata de casa y se veía rejuvenecida, ahora luciendo una larga trenza que le caía por encima del hombro. Me dio su sonrisa de valentía y un adiós.

Al alejarme en el carro, me volteé para ver por última vez su jardín bien cuidado con la vieja tendedera—su tendido vestido floreado ondeaba en la brisa.

UN MOMENTO

My mother's parents came from Cuba in the early days, when relations were still very good. America wanted anything Cuba had to offer: its food, music, dances and even its people. My grandmother lived into her 90's in a little house in Ybor City. She raised ten children and never learned to speak English. Or, should I say, she never *had* to speak English. At the corner store, the hospital, the bakery, the drug store, they all spoke her language. She talked to us grandchildren in Spanish and although I did not speak it well, we worked together to communicate the basics of love and life.

It always bugged me that I never learned to speak Spanish fluently or even better. My mother spoke it beautifully; my father spoke Spanish and Italian! But, me? I just learned the basics: cuss words, ordering food and descriptions of female anatomy.

I dreamed that someday it would be revealed to me, all clear and available and I could carry on a decent conversation in at least one of the languages of my family's heritage. Ironically, that redemption came in the form of my little Cuban grandmother.

I'd been away for a while and hadn't seen *Abuela* in several years. All her children were long grown and gone. She insisted on living alone, a tiny sweet, kind-hearted old woman in an area that had been going downhill for years.

I headed into the neighborhood, went by *La Segunda*

and got some Cuban bread. I drove by Cuscaden Park, past the water tower and the hospital and there on the corner across from Shirley Ann's Grocery was my grandmother's little wood-frame house. I knocked lightly on the screen door expecting her surprised greeting, *¿Abuela?* No response. Peering through the screen, I noticed her standing still in the middle of the room. A little concerned, I slipped in and walked up calling her name again.

Abuelita had always been tiny, not even five feet tall and her once jet black hair was now shot through with silver and grey. She usually wore it in a long braid down the middle of her back or wrapped around her head and pinned up. Today, it was spread out in a long fan all the way to her feet. With motes of dust glinting in sunlight surrounding her, she looked like a saint from a holy card. And, she still wasn't moving or saying anything.

Hola, abuela. ¿Como estas? ¿Bien? Still no answer, something wasn't right. She didn't seem to even know I was there. I tried again. *¿Abuelita, esta bien?* When she spoke in her sweet Spanish, somehow I understood.

"I'm 93...two weeks ago.... I was 23! We were walking on the *Malecon* and the waves were so high, we tried to run, my friends and I... but the water sprayed us. We got so wet.... our hair... all over our dresses...mine was covered in camellias, so pretty....we laughed and laughed... we we're going to..."

At this, she faltered. A little lost and a little sad. I don't think I had ever seen her sad before. I smiled down at that familiar face, her pale eyes as blue as the far away sea in her mind. And then, slowly, she raised her tiny hand to my cheek and answered, *"Si, muy bien."*

Relieved, I gave her a big hug, she felt so frail. I walked her over to the couch where we sat for a long time just holding hands, smiling at each other, asking simple questions. The words just came to me like a memory, I had always known, but could not speak them until I was grown.

Finally, the time came and I kissed her cheek

goodbye. *Abuelita* followed me out onto the creaky old porch. She'd put on a robe and seemed refreshed, braiding her long hair over one shoulder.
She gave me that brave smile and a little wave.

Driving away, I turned back for a last look at her neat yard with the old clothes line. My grandmother's flowered dress swaying in the breeze.

ABOUT FACE

Did you ever know someone, who knew exactly what they wanted to be ever since they were a little kid? And, did you just *happen* to be there at the exact moment that they made this life-defining decision? For me, it was with my childhood friend, Little Albert, at the Tampa Theatre, Saturday afternoon, spending the day watching war movies. We were around ten.

Local legend has it that when Albert was five years old, his dad took the family to New York City on a vacation. At the Empire State Building on the observation platform near the top, people were lining the guard railings taking in the view, when Big Albert picked up his young son and swung him out over the railing, holding him out into thin air.

While Little Albert dangled in mid-air, 1000 feet above the city streets, kicking his feet like crazy and clawing at his father's strong arms, his dad just smiled the whole time, even with his wife screaming at him like a banshee. Then, he lightly swung Albert back to safety and put him down with a pat on his head saying, "Now, the rest of his life won't seem so hard."

Albert and I had known each other since first grade and used to spend every Saturday we could at the Tampa Theatre.

I would have to start working my dad for the money the night before. It was like picking my way through a minefield. Dad sitting back in his easy chair, holding the newspaper up like a shield, his face set in stone, looking kind of like Jimmy Durante…if Durante was playing a character in the Godfather! And me, standing in front of him in a stance that said, "Please, sir, can I have some more?"

"Whaddya need?" he'd grunt and then quickly add, "Bare necessities." Trust me, it was not fun. The wrong inflection, a shift in attitude, anything, really, could have dire consequences, leading to a total Sicilian shutdown. No response, no expression, no chance. And, if you persisted, there would be the dropping of the paper and the lurch from the chair. Whoa, I'd rather ask a bear for money!

"Ten cents for the bus both ways and 25 cents for the double feature; it's a great movie this week, Pop; it's got Gina Lollobrigida!" Then, there would be a long silence, another grunt and a rustle of the paper which was the signal that I should stop babbling and get in my final figures, "Small popcorn's only 15 cents and I can drink water, Pop; I don't really need the ten cents for a soda."

My dad would make a solemn affair of doling out the exact amount; turning over the coins and scrutinizing them, shooting me a glare now and then, as if I needed reminding that I was such a burden. It would often be a little short; times were hard and there were five kids, so I tried hard to still be grateful and not look disappointed. I know now, it was his way of character building. Sometimes, in the morning, my mother would give me another dime. Aw, mom…you were the finest.

But, unlike all the other things that I bugged my dad for, this was different… because to him, this was like giving to the church. Tampa Theatre was always treated as a place of reverence in my family.

My Dad loved to tell the story of his family moving here from Kankakee, so his father could work on the Tampa Theatre, one of the great American Movie Palaces, a Historic Landmark for all time. For me and my family, it will always be a lasting tribute of these humble craftsmen from another place and time, offering up their old world talents and fashioning something beautiful and lasting in their new world. That's probably the only reason that I was allowed to go downtown all by myself because he knew right where I'd be, all day long.

Buying your ticket from the lady in the little glass booth and then walking through those doors into the cool air, up the red carpet onto that incredible tile floor and the great concession stand, I mean, Wow! Most everyone would be talking in hushed tones, like it was a special place for them, too. Man, just a great place to do your growing up.

One week, we watched John Garfield as a war hero in the *Pride of the Marines,* and we were blown away! He was so different from any actor we had seen before. Albert loved that Garfield was small but tough and smart, too. So, he insisted we sit through the whole thing again. And after that, what the hell, one more time! When we finally came out, it was almost dark and Little Albert looked around as if seeing the world with new eyes and loudly declared to the rest of Franklin Street, "That's what I want to be... a Marine!" From that moment on, my little buddy never faltered from that decision. All through grade school, whenever the question came up,
"Albert, what you are going to be when you grow up?"
"A Marine!"
In junior high, "Hey, you going out for any sports?"
"Naw, I'm gonna be a Marine!"
And later, in high school,
"Albert, you going to go to college?" "Nope! Marines."

We all laughed but also knew that he damn well meant it. Truth was we admired his conviction. It was the early 60's and we were all so confused about hippies and heroes. But, not Albert, he had no doubts.

After the movies, we loved to haunt the Army/Navy store just outside of downtown. We would spend long hours rummaging through the aisles, trying on uniforms, checking out gas masks, bayonets and parachutes, hefting grenades. There was always something new to discover there. Albert would buy himself patches, *1st Marine Division,* and sew them on his backpack. Everybody got their backpacks at Army/Navy in those days.

Later, riding home on the Nebraska Avenue bus, Albert and I would replay the movie we had just seen, getting all excited again, talking weapons, like the BAR, the .45

Machine gun or the bazooka. We'd comment on the actors' moves and attitude,
"You believe those guys on that patrol?"
"Yeah, they were grouped way too close together, one mortar woulda take 'em all out!"

Then, as soon as we stepped off the bus, the next few blocks would be our war zone, *Iwo Jima! Battle of the Bulge!* Little Albert was a big student of military history and loved to read inspiring stories of war heroes. So, he would call out where we were and what we were doing, like, Guadalcanal, closing in on the Japs! Hitting the beachheads at Anzio!
He taught me all the hands signals:
Watch me, Stay low,
Take cover,
Double-time.

Weaving in and out of bushes to avoid fire and then taking cover behind trees to return fire, we had each other's backs and were always ready to take one for the Corps! Albert would always be *Gung Ho* for charging the enemy machine gun nest. I'd set it up for him lobbing some grenades, then as the smoke and dust cleared, we'd be up and firing on the run. *Serpentine, serpentine!*

Usually, my buddy took one in the leg or shoulder but would find a way to stagger painfully up to the enemy position and then clear them out. And, whenever, I got wounded and was lying there, Albert would be right by my side, helping me up, "Put your arm on my shoulder. I got you, *salvaje!*" He used to call me *salvaje*. It means savage because I was so big, well, at least, compared to him, but it was also a little tongue in cheek because he knew I was just a teddy bear.

Albert had even learned to speak German just from watching the TV show *Combat* because they used subtitles. There was a favorite ploy that he would use; he'd pretend he was an enemy soldier that had been wounded, "*Ich bin erschossen!*" He'd cry in pain and when a second German, also played by Albert asked, "*Wo bist du?*" Albert would spring up and say, "Right here, Kraut!" Spraying him with machine gun fire and laughing like a crazy man.

Finally it was Graduation Day and as soon as Albert turned 18 that summer, it was *Semper Fi* time. The boys went out with him the night before to the House of Blue Lights and got trashed toasting the little man and his dreams finally coming true. Sentimental and sloshed, we ended up at the Pancake House, of course, and then drove Little Albert to the recruiting office. The year was 1968.

Downtown Tampa at 6:00 on a Sunday morning was like a ghost town, not a soul in sight, not even a wino. But when we drove up, there was someone in the recruiting office, all right....a Marine sat ramrod straight behind a counter drinking coffee and doing some paperwork. Albert had planned on signing up and then heading back home to start packing his gear.

Through the glass, we watched him walk in and talk to the Marine who stood up, towering over Little Albert. The Marine listened then shook his head. Albert protested. The Marine crossed his arms over his chest and gave the smallest of head shakes. At this, the little guy lost it... became incensed, was actually jumping up and down, yelling. He looked like a cartoon! The Marine just looked at the door and believe me, that was enough.

Our buddy finally gave up, turned around and stormed out, a man defeated. We couldn't believe it, I mean, what the hell!

Apparently, the Marine had told him, without even the benefit of a measuring tape, that Little Albert would not meet the height requirement necessary for the US Marines.

Still pretty drunk, we became a little belligerent as we comforted our friend.

"Jarheads don't know who they're messin' with."

"Don't worry, man, we're gonna get you into that damn Corps."

And then, *someone* came up with an idea and convinced Albert that he could make himself taller if he really, really, really tried. It wasn't me, I know what you're thinking, but it wasn't me. It wasn't! OK, it was me, but I was just trying to give my buddy some comfort in his time of need. And, Albert jumped at the chance. Man, did he ever!

Little Albert did some research and found out that, in truth, he was only 3/4 of an inch too short for the Marines. Determined that he could stretch himself, somehow and make it, he dove in to action. First, he put up a bar in his room so he could hang for long periods of time. Then, every single thing he owned went up on high shelves, even his toothbrush, so all day long, he had to reach and stretch. The seat went back in his car and the rear view mirror angled higher.

He began training every single day and this was way before the movie Rocky and people were running marathons and stuff like that. All day long, Albert imagined himself growing taller and taller, the bones in his spine stretching and lengthening; he was actually using visualization long before it was a happening thing.

To say the least, we were all impressed. We'd never known anyone with such single-minded purpose. It was like, through the sheer force of his will and determination, he could change that one little part of himself and... be *little*, no more.

Someone advised Albert that you grow while you sleep, so he began socking in the ZZZs. Sleeping and stretching, sleeping and stretching! The night before the big day came and Albert slept in his clothes and in the morning we carried him out lying down flat on a board and slid him into the back of my father's station wagon. He had heard that you're always taller in the morning and was, wisely, going to maximize this potential. At the office, we carried him on the board to the door, eased him down and watched him walk tall into the building.

Albert made it by the thinnest of red hairs, 1/16 of an inch, but... He made it! The little guy was floating on air when he got to the last table. There, a recruiting officer stamped his paperwork and handed him the file. On the cover in big red letters was the word: *REJECTED*. Albert was floored, in denial, he stammered, "But... I did it... I made the height!" Without even looking up the Marine said, "Yeah, but you failed the IQ test, Bud!"

Albert would never be a Marine.

Well, he ranted and raved all the way home. And being good friends we ranted and raved right along with him. At his house, Big Albert came out to greet his son expectantly. When told the bad news, his father took a long beat, slowly nodding his head, "Well, you know, son, even though I had mixed feelings about the whole thing, I realize how much it meant to you. I'm so sorry. Come on, everybody inside, let's have a beer!"

We were all so close 100 years ago, so tight. Nothing else like it. And then, in baby steps, we moved apart.

I saw Albert for the first time in forever during the 7th inning stretch at a Rays game. I was up doing the look-around. Love when I see someone that I know, usually somebody from Ybor or West Tampa. Baseball was huge back then before football muscled it out. Even if I can't dredge up their name, I remember the face and they seem to recognize me, too. So we give each other the head nod and smile. This time, though, I had no problem putting a name to the face and I headed down the steps with a big grin.

Albert and I shook hands in the old style with thumbs crossed and hands clasped, a token of camaraderie that I dearly miss. He wasn't so little anymore. He'd grown quite a bit and looked in great shape just like his Dad.

When we started talking family and found out that we both had sons, I asked, expectantly "You want him to be a Marine?" "Hell, No!" Albert answered, "Those days are over, *Salvaje*!"

"Did you know that since the *Great War*, there have been over one *hundred million* people killed by men fighting some silly ass war or other?"

"No way, man," I replied, "you're kidding."

"I wish I was, brother," Albert said soberly, "I wish I was. And, we're talking mostly civilians here, old folks, women and children. Children, man, children!"

"No!"

He reaffirmed his voice thick with emotion. "I'd never want any son of mine to add to all the misery already in the world!"

We gave each other a big hug, promised to keep in touch and I headed back to my seat. Shaking my head and thinking…How proud I was of my old friend.

Neighborhood

I thought my Dad would live forever. He seemed invulnerable. He had worked hard all his life, seldom showing the strain of the toll that kind of labor can take. In his eighties, he was still healthy, strong and happy as usual. Then, he got the flu and when I saw him a week later, I barely recognized him. He ended up in St. Joseph's, and since we knew that his time was coming to an end, we tried to make sure there was someone there who loved him at all times.

As he started to slip, he began muttering a lot and was restless, so much so, that he had to be restrained. He kept repeating that he had to get back to the neighborhood. I had been going by to spend time with him. Once, just as I got there, he leans over and whispers, "I gotta go." Thinking he meant the bathroom, I get him up and roll his IV in, where he stands in front of the toilet, lost and looking up at me. When did he get so small? This time he added, "I gotta go, neighborhood!" It became my father's mantra. And to tell you the truth, for the rest of the short time he had left, he said little else. Dark eyes pleading, he'd whisper, "Neighborhood." Good times flitting cross his mind, he'd chuckle, "Neighborhood!" Forceful and impatient, a glimmer of his old fierceness, he would demand, "Neighborhood!" Sometimes I'd encourage him, stroking his hair, "That was the best damn neighborhood there ever was, dad." And he'd agree, "Goddam right!"

I wasn't there when he died… but if there were any last words, I know what they were. We laid him next to my mother and sister, surrounded by friends and family both present and passed on.

A few weeks later, I begged off a theater after party and feeling too restless to go right back across the bay. I took the old home route again, past the water tower and the Old Peoples' Home to 23rd Avenue. Slowly cruising down the real memory lane, I took in all the familiar places, remembering the people who lived there, playing in those yards.

Our old house was on the next corner, I coast to a stop and look out the car window and…it's gone! Nothing left but the little stoop of red bricks my dad had made while I handed him tools. I was so surprised that I had to look around just to make sure I was in the right place. I mean what the hell! So I got out and walked around, making my way through the weeds, kicking rocks, working my all the way back to the alley and nothing, not one little bit of the place was left. Everything gone!

The azaleas surrounding the house that my dad had nurtured so lovingly, coaxing the blooms of white and pink; the tall hedges of cherry laurel he sculpted so carefully that people watching him work, would jokingly ask, "Dick, could you give me a little trim around the ears when you're done?"

Gone too, was the backyard patio that we had built using paving stones salvaged from the sidewalks of Ybor just before the earth movers scooped them all up when I-4 tore through the neighborhood on its way to see "Mickey." There was nothing, no trace left of what we once had.

Later that night, sitting on the edge of bed, my wife

turns to me out of sleep to ask how everything went. I tell her instead about the house being gone. Quiet for a long while in the dark, I thought she had gone back to sleep, then yawning she asks, "What do you think happened to it?" Musing, I answered, "I think he took it with him!" Turning back over, she responded, "Well, if anyone could do it, your dad could."

That night I had a dream. My father was pushing an old wooden wheelbarrow up a steep and rocky hill. And perched precariously with one of its corners fit into that wheelbarrow was our old house, towering into the air. His big gnarled hands were on the handles and he was leaning into them, cords of muscle standing out on his back and shoulders, as he guided his burden around boulders and over mounds of dirt and rocks. Sometimes, sliding backwards as he lost his footing on loose pebbles, he would pause to balance his load, dig in and with a dogged grunt, heave at it, again and again, forward, further, up! Always with his eyes on the prize and always with my father's attitude, "It's not heavy…it's not far."

Finally, he is there, where he wants to be. Gently, oh so carefully, he lowers his precious cargo. He checks that it's secured on its foundation. Level and plumb. Done. Then, he goes inside to clean up. What my Dad would refer to as the 3 *S's*. Shower, shave and shampoo. He comes out all smelling of after-shave with his hair slicked back wet. Wearing a fresh clean *camisetta* and comfortable work pants, he heads to the kitchen to tend his sauce. There's a big pot of red sauce steaming on the stove spreading the aromas of garlic, basil and oregano.

In the hallway, my sister, Cynthia, is chatting on the phone, lounging in a chair with her feet up, just like one of the girls from *Bye, Bye Birdie*. My mom is in her place at the kitchen table, sipping Cuban coffee from a china cup and leafing through a magazine. And my dad, with a dish towel draped over one shoulder is stirring his sauce, tasting it. Adding a little bit a this and a little bit a that. He's singing, soft and low, almost to himself. Something kinda sweet…maybe, something from the Hit Parade…something like…

♫*Gonna take a Sentimental Journey,*
Sentimental Journey Home
Gonna take a sentimental journey
♫*To renew old memories.*

El Lector

"I can't believe him! What is he thinking?" the younger daughter, Vilma asks, hands on her hips.

"He's got a lot on his mind," her older sister, Stella replies. "I'm not so sure." Vilma answers. "What do you mean? You're not so sure. Don't be like that!" Vilma says, as she works to set the breakfast table.

"It's like nothing has changed and everything's just as it's always been!"

"I don't know what you expect him to do," Stella answers from the kitchen.

"Something!" says her sister, "Yell, scream, laugh…anything!"

"Oh, he laughs." Vilma reassures her, still bustling from room to room. "That's never going to stop."
"You know sometimes, I wonder if he's even aware of what's going on." Stella muses through narrowed eyes.
"He's not senile!" Vilma replies as she heads for the kitchen, "He's as sharp as ever."

Cornering her sister, Stella asks, "Do you think it could be… that he really doesn't know?" "Oh, please! He knows!" says her sister confidently.

Lost in thought, Stella stubbornly shakes her head. "I'm not so sure. I'd like to be but I'm just not."

Both women quickly stop talking, as their father enters, takes his place at the table and settles himself. The sisters finish serving coffee and breakfast in a strained silence, finally broken as the father comments, between sips of his *café con leche,*

"That's what I like," he begins nodding his head, "women who have the wisdom and good graces to be quiet until a man has had his first cup of coffee in the morning."

The sisters move away, letting their father eat in peace and they begin to talk shop. "Do you believe that leaf they've been giving us? What crap!" One starts and her sister agrees, *"Dios mio!"* I had 5 or 10 just fall apart before I finished them. It was so dry. I never got them into the mold. It's embarrassing!"

They both shake their heads in distress, "as long as we don't have to work with the *maduro.*

"The last time, it made me sick for days. I don't care if I never roll that leaf again. I leave that to the men!" *"Sí, claro,"* Vilma agrees then adds "The other day, coming home, I was passing *El Parque,* when I saw a man lighting up a *breva* and he was having a helluva time getting it going.

Then, he sees me and gives me this look, like it was my fault. Men and their cigars. Humph!"

"Never forget, girls," their father intones from his place at the table, "It's all about the cigars!"

"Well, since you brought up the subject, do you have any plans? Vilma wants to know." "Yes, I do," their father answers, nodding. The women wait, expectantly, as they look back and forth at each other and their father who seems to be enjoying this.

Finally, breaking his silence, he announces, "I plan on getting a haircut and a shave and then a shoe shine! By the time I get to the factory, I am going to look like Ramon Navarro!" Vilma snaps, "And then what?"

Gesturing vaguely, her father answers, "Then, I'll do what I always do." "And, afterward?" she presses him. "Afterward. I do so love the way you choose your words, mija," the father chuckles. "I find it so…"

Stella, the peacemaker offers, "Papu, I think what she's trying to say is…" "Why does she have to try?" Their father interrupts. "Can't she just say it?"

Enunciating every word deliberately, Vilma confronts him, "What –are- you- going- to- do- with- yourself *afterward?* And, then hastens to add, "And, don't just say, "I'll come home!

"Ah, so much like your mother!" The father muses, "I love talking to you two because it reminds me so much of her. I am so glad to have you both here with me."

"Don't start with that!" Vilma snaps. "You're just avoiding the question and I don't want to hear that 'I changed your diapers thing' that you always do either!"

"Changed your diapers?" He comes right back, "Chica, I cut your damn cord! I am the reason you are walking around free!"

"We love having you here, too." Stella begins, looking to her sister, "it's just that…well… we're worried about you." The father's face softens as he looks at his children. Then, in that voice that all fathers use, he answers. "Aw, do you want to sit on my lap while I read, like you used to when you were a little girls? Trust me. I am going to be fine. Don't give it a second thought. You have your own lives, now. Live them. Or," he offers, playfully "if you like, we can go together to get Cuban toast, like we used to. We can go back in the kitchen and watch them make it."

Dreamily, Stella adds, "I love to see them spread the butter. They always have so much! It's like a whole mountain of butter." And they only spread it one way!" adds their father.

"I'm sorry to break this up but" Vilma interrupts a little on edge.

"Yes, of course, "What will I do…what *will* I do?" the father answers, looking up in thought until he comes upon an idea, "I can sharpen knives!" Triumphant, he explains, "*Chavetas.* It's a good job. I have a lot of experience sharpening things."

"What experience?" Vilma snaps then holds her finger up to his face. "You have experience in one thing and one thing only!"

"Well" the father explains, "I have been sharpening

81

minds and tongues for years according to *Los Patrones*. How hard could knives be?"

"Vilma! That's not true!" Stella comes to her father's defense. "There's probably nothing he couldn't do, if he wanted to!"

"Well, w*hat* do you *want* to do?" she asks again.

He leans back in his chair and grins, "I am going to live like an Italian!" "Oh, please!" the girls cry in frustration. "Really, Papu", her sister says, "This is serious." The father takes a long beat and the girls are hoping it's all over when he asks, quite seriously.

"Do you know what Beethoven *said* when they asked him what *he* was going to do, now that he would soon be deaf?

"I don't care what he said." Vilma shoots back. "Stay with us here, Papu." The girls plead. Unfazed, the father continues, "He said, 'I shall seize Fate by the throat. It will not overcome me!'"

Stamping her foot, Stella nearly screams "You're not Beethoven!"

"She's right" her sister agrees, "We're a family. These are decisions and plans that a family has to make and deal with. These things are important to us. And, you're talking Beethoven!"

Brooding quietly for a while, he finally relents, "All right. What do you want to know?" The sisters look at each other in relief and tentatively, begin, "Is there any way that things could stay the same?" "No!" The father affirms. "Could you work at another factory?" Stella asks. "Sorry, but, no," the father answers, hastening to add, "It is not my decision, you know. *Los Patrones* and the unions, they call the shots."

"Why? *They* don't even pay you. The workers are the ones that pay you!" Vilma replies with her sister adding, "You can't even get paid inside. You have to go outside to get it, like it's a crime." Near tears, her sister comments, "And, all they left you is that little chair to sit on; it's shameful."

"That was probably their intent," The father sighs. "I told you, it's all about the cigars; nothing else matters. Like so often happens, the big shots are really not that different from us. We come from similar places with similar upbringing, but with success and money comes change and not always for the good. Here, it's been one crisis after another and I'm sorry to say that cool heads did not prevail. So, I play the fool to keep from going to war."

"We've known so many of the bosses for years," the girls begin. "We went to school with their children. I just don't get it." At a loss for an answer, they are both quiet.

"Everything is changing so fast," the father begins. "Look at all that has happened. Cheap cigars, cigarettes! I don't know how people can smoke those things. A quality product made by hand is not what people want anymore. Look around, my loves. Everybody is struggling just to get by. Years ago, we were producing millions of Spanish hand-made cigars, millions! We rolled 100 million for every man, woman and child in Tampa. Quality was the main focus, not volume. The strike did nothing but make it worse, then, another strike *and* a lockout. *Los Patrones* misguidedly felt that they had to let people go.

Then, for whatever reasons, they chose mostly the loyal workers who had brought them all their success in the first place. Maybe to show them who's boss, who knows? We were left staring at doors with bars on them and people were starving! It was the time of the *cocina economica*. We never really recovered. Eventually they opened the doors again but they brought in machines which produced an inferior product twice as fast and for half the cost."

"Se acabó."

"So, everyone's dream of a house and a family," Vilma asks. "What becomes of that? Are they all going to lose it, now?"

"No," the father answers. "But, they will have to find another way to get it."

"But, the protests at the Labor Temple, all those people!"

Stella remarks near tears. "We hoped that would convince *somebody* that what is going on is wrong!" "I did as well," their father quietly replies, "But, unfortunately," he shrugs,
"It was the death knell. Girls," the father begins calmly, "it will all work out. Trust me. We have always been so close and that we will always remain, come what may.

Those were such wonderful times. Your mother would always be worried that I was filling your head with ideas unbecoming to young ladies. And, I would answer that I would never be able to change whatever you two would become and how much I was looking forward to it."

"You know, Papu," Stella begins, "we always hoped that you might meet someone, someday. You know, just for some company, maybe, someone from work. You know so many people. It would be so nice to have a ..."

"I try," the father interrupts, "Occasionally, I really do. I love women, dearly, talking to them, their wonderful smell. I still do *La Septima* Walk. I love to look or chat, maybe even flirt a little. But my heart is not in it...Thirty years of marital bliss with your mother," he says with a faraway look in his eyes. "I don't need anything more."

"Change is good!" Vilma says. "You taught us that. Now, you're not willing?"

"Not to worry," their father reassures them. "I have plenty to do. Baseball games, boxing. There's dancing at the Cuban Club. I'll always play dominoes. Tell you the truth; I'm looking forward to it all. Oh, I'm not done; I'll still be speaking my mind, that's never going to stop. But, now, I can do it whenever and wherever I like. You know, it's silly but I feel the same as I always have. I'm very lucky. Deep down inside, I don't think that I'm much different than I ever was. Yet, sometimes, I will be strolling down the street, happy-go-lucky, and then I catch a glimpse of someone staring back at me, reflected in a café window and...I'll feel that I..." Then finishing cheerfully, he adds, *"Bueno, me voy!"*

His girls encircle him and El Lector warmly says "I want you both to know that I do appreciate your love and concern."

The girls answer, "Thanks for indulging us. We'll see you later. We are so proud of you; don't ever forget that."

"I won't and thank you." The Lector says slipping into his jacket and shooting his cuffs on his way out the door.

The women sit in the silence, and then Stella asks sweetly, "Vilma, would you get me a cup of coffee, please?" Picking up the cups from the table and heading into the kitchen, Stella says to no one in particular, "Whew! Arguing with a hard-headed Spaniard is exhausting!" Arching her brow, her sister replies, "humph!" Stella sits for a while, shaking her head before throwing up her hands and exclaiming in disbelief. "Beethoven!"

The Lector fires up one of his favorite cigars as he turns onto the sidewalk with its familiar paving stones. He strolls into a storefront and greets the man behind the counter heartily, "*Y que*, Sammy?" The well-dressed man returns the warmth with a big smile, "*La misma mierda.*"

"Did those spats that I liked come in?" asks the Lector, looking down at the cases. "*Lo siento*, Don Emiliano, they won't be here until next week. You wanted the fawn, no?"

"*Si, gracias,*" The Lector replies as Sammy calls him over to the counter. *Sotto voce*, he begins "I figured you might appreciate this," opening a large grey ledger.

"Two men came in the other day, never seen them before. They heard that they could get something *en fiado* - on credit. One got a tie and the other a belt. I wrote the items in the book then showed it to them and told them where to sign. The first one picks up the pencil and looks at the page for a while and then signs his name, *Jose sin peso.*" "*Comico!*" chuckles The Lector showing his amusement but Sammy pauses and holds up his finger and continues. "Then, he gives the pencil to his friend who looks at the page, then back at his friend, and then he signs *his* name *Mario con el!*" The two friends laugh out loud and the Lector asks, "*Guajiros? Por su puesto!*" his friend answers. "*De montes.*" Still smiling, the Lector turns to leave, shaking his head. "*Que rico*! I am going to use that today."   Sammy's smile is just a little strained as he watches his old friend strolling out the door.

Back out on the sidewalk, the traffic is picking up adding to the usual smells of coffee, cigar smoke and fumes from the streetcar. The Lector greets people along the way and gets horns and shouts. With his usual aplomb, he acknowledges them all. Finished with his errands, he heads to the factory. Once there, holding onto the railing at the front steps, he pauses and looks fondly all the way up, then begins to climb.

He crosses the floor, conscious of all the factories he has worked in during his time and feeling a little more emotional than he thought he would. Surprising, he thinks as he turns the corner to one of his favorite places: a small alcove where the workers go to sharpen their knives, as they have been for decades. The whetstone, standing as big as a man must have been considerably bigger at one time. But, now was riddled with gouges, dips, cuts and slices from generations of *tabaqueros* honing their blades.

With a last pat to the stone, he turns to the old wooden stairs and heads up, up to the *galleria,* the rolling floor*,* where the workers ply their trade and the magic happens. Tobacco dust glints in the light streaming through the windows, as men, women and even some children sit at row after row of long wooden tables, quietly working: rolling, bunching and cutting.

 El Lector arrives. He sees the workers gathered together in front of a small table, and when they notice him, everyone freezes, suddenly uncomfortable. As they slowly move away from the table, El Lector realizes what was getting their attention. There, on a small wooden table stood something no one in the factory ever thought they would see: A radio.

A good looking young man awkwardly blurts out, "We were going to knock it off the table and smash it."

"Don't do that!" El Lector jokes, "Then we won't be able to listen to the ball game."

"Well, what should we do with it?" An older woman nervously asks, wringing her hands.

"Nothing," he assures them; "It doesn't belong to us."

The workers reluctantly move back to their places. A small wiry man with a big grin greets El Lector with a warm handshake, "Caballero, I have something for you from everybody," as he shows an envelope tucked into his pocket. El Lector trying to look natural, replies "Are you crazy? You're not supposed to do that here!" Augustine, smiling through a big cigar in the corner of his mouth, quotes, "Let Hercules do what he may, eh?" "Damn" the Lector chuckles, "You have learned well." Obviously, pleased with the compliment, his friend changes the subject. "What do you think you will do with all that time on your hands?" Beaming, the Lector answers, "I am going to live like an Italian!"

"*Como?*" Augustine is thrown, so the Lector explains, "The Italians have a saying; it's really a way of life. *Dolce far niente!* Have you ever heard that?"

"Can't say that I have," says his friend. "Sweet, uh, something?"

"Very good, my friend! It means, 'How sweet, to do nothing!' Good, Eh?" Augustine is pleased, "Damn, now I envy you. Just remember it when your time comes." His friend smiles, stands up and gestures to the group of workers then turns to the Lector, "Los *tabaqueros* have something they would like to tell you."

Looking over Augustine's shoulder, he sees the workers slowly shuffling towards him, heads humbly down. A big roguish man with jet-black hair recites, "Thank you for The Count of Monte Cristo, it gave me hope." Then another adds, "You always gave us the baseball news; Babe Ruth, Lou Gehrig, the Yankees were my favorite." Then what appeared to be two sisters stepped up with matching smiles, "We loved the *Marianela*; you made it so romantic; it took me away." Gushes the first one, while the other giggles, "and Sancho

Panza, you were so funny acting like him!"
You taught so many good sayings, "*El tiempo todo lo cura,*"
"Yes," El Lector replies, "Time heals all."
A small dark man, who looks like a boxer and sounds like a foghorn is very serious when he confesses, "I felt so sorry for The Hunchback with his eternal love."
"Ah, *Si!* So sad, but so very beautiful."
" It was like you had lit a candle for us. Thank you so much."
El Lector gathers them around him with arms open saying, "I am so moved by your gratitude and your generosity. But, never forget that each one of you learned everything that you did because you listened and remembered. Many of you also helped your friends and family who did not work in the factory by sharing all the stories and knowledge that you heard here. That, I believe is the most valuable thing that we have accomplished during our time together. We created something lasting and important, and I am very proud of all of you."

There was applause and shouts with the workers banging their knives on the tables to show their appreciation for the longest time. El Lector was moved at the outpouring. Quieting everyone, he takes his seat and directs them, "Now, it's time to get to work." And, opening his book, he begins.

It was the best of times;
It was the worst of times...

Some had heard the words before. And, many have heard the words since that fateful day. All agreed they had never heard El Lector in such a fine voice.

The words carried into the rafters and wooden beams of the factory. Light and airy like wisps of smoke they rose. Slowly, at first but steadily up and up, then out the open windows they poured. Rich and full, like coffee, they spread to the squares and the streets. People passing began to slow and stop to listen. More gathered, heads bent and ears cocked to every word. They seemed to forget where they were going, what they were doing. But, all shared a look on their faces. It was a look of intent, of joy and wonder, which began to shift from person to person. Man, woman, child, all found the reason to suspend themselves for the moment and for the duration of that moment, to simply listen. Little was spoken, lest they talk over the words and miss something. And, rather than move away, they gathered closer, quietly using a shared body language to find their place and settle.

The sun was soft and cool on the listeners as they stood in the open air. Traffic on the street, both in cars and on foot, softened as well, not wanting to intrude on the moment. The words were flitting about now higher and higher, some soaring even to the heights.

THE MIDWIFE OF YBOR

Maria sits on a bentwood chair at a round table on the wrought iron balcony overlooking 7th Avenue, her head bent into a small circle of light from the lamp in cool still dark morning. She treasured this quiet time after what was usually a noisy night. Her journal was a small notebook where she wrote in pencil in her native Sicilian the salient facts of her work;

Name of the father, His occupation and age
Name of the mother
Her age and number of live births and how many lost
Name of the new child
How she is paid by individual or social club

Orange and ruby clouds of the illuminated sunrise streak up behind cigar factory towers. She notices the street lights going off one by one. She thinks back to when she first arrived in Ybor. She and the city were both so young! In those days the street were of dirt and the gas men who kept the street lights going were her first friends as she hurried through the town at all hours of the day and night.

Now, the lights are electric and she had an automobile. She is the first woman in Tampa to drive her own machine. She knows her husband put up with a lot of teasing from his companions at the Italian Club because of it.

Smiling to herself, she knew he did not take these taunts to heart. He was, in fact, very proud of and madly in love with her.

One of the secrets to their happy marriage had been established soon after she arrived in America from Italy. No matter what hour she would arrive home, he would awake and take her into his arms. After all the many hours another woman's labor might take, Maria found herself never weary. Instead, she would be filled with passion at the brilliance of new life! Her young husband had been very surprised that her zeal for her work would be for him as well.

Good man that he was, he also understood her pain when a child had been lost and held her even more tenderly at those times. Never wanting to add to the grieving mother's pain, she sobbed her own sense of loss alone with her man who understood.

Now a small bell rings next to her desk. It is hooked up to a sign next to the door so that the whole house or street is not awakened when she is called. Maria looks longingly at the door to her bedroom and then heads downstairs. There is a woman from the neighborhood that she knows and has been expecting.

"Señora, please, you must come now. My niece, Encarnacion Cueto; it is her time."

"Then it is my time as well," Maria answers as she picks up her bag from beside the door. She and Ana hustle go to her car and head across to the other side of town.

"Enca is so frightened." The woman begins. "Her mother, my blessed sister, died giving birth to her. I know she thinks that will happen to her."

"Every mother, every time, is afraid. Yet here we are." The Midwife calmly replies, setting her tone and her spirit for the journey ahead. "Si, claro, pero, every woman knows she might have to give her life for her child," Ana says "And that doesn't stop once they are outside of you either, eh?" They laugh together easily. Maria has a daughter of her own now, her heart's delight.

Ana chatters on nervous and excited, "I love my niece like my own child. But she chooses a man that her father does not like. He is Italian. That makes things difficult. I don't understand these men with their politics and pretenses. He works side by side with Italians in the cigar factor yet because we are Cuban she cannot marry such a man? No comprendo!"

Maria quickly changes the subject. "Ana, the dress you made for me is very beautiful. It fits so well, comfortable and still stylish. You do such good work; I am proud to wear it to the Italian Club for Fiesta." Ana is pleased, "For your help with my niece, I would gladly make you ten dresses. Better than that chicken the Cacciatore's gave you that turned out to be the loudest rooster in Ybor!" They laugh again as Maria parks in front of a casita. "Did your husband like it Señora?"

"Like it! He chased me around the kitchen for a stolen kiss. Si, Si, he liked it very much. One lovely dress is plenty. She is young and strong and has her wise Tia besides her to make my job easier."

Three small girls sit on the stairs of the front porch, as Ana rushes ahead inside. The middle girl speaks up.

"I know who you are", she says with the savvy only a child can show. Maria laughs, "And who are you?"

"I'm Vilma and these are my sisters Stella and Beba. You are bringing Enca's baby."
"Si, such a smart child!
And, how do you know this?"
"Because, you bring it in your bag! I saw it at our house when you brought us Beba and Felina!"

Maria bends down to kiss the small head, saying "And you little angel, is why I do this day after day and night after night."

She then goes inside what will be her place of work for the next 8 to 24 hours. Inside the young mother lays on a

small bed, tossing and turning, colorful pillows and blankets
are strewn all around her. She moans out in pain. "Stay
strong Mommi, I am here now. Your Tia caught me just
before I went to sleep. From one end of Ybor to the other,
the bambinos keep coming. More babies than cigars these
days I think." As she speaks, she examines the young woman
girl, finally takes a long wooden scope from her bag and
places it on the mother's belly. She listens carefully.

"Very good!" Maria announces, "You are almost
there and your baby is facing the right way, *es muy importatnte*.
You are open just right. This is going to be a good birth."
This reassures the young woman, and she now lies quietly as
the pain subsides.

"Señora Maria, we gathered all the things like you
told us to do." Encarnacion, still stunned from the last pain,
gasps, "Eiee! It starts so suddenly and then stops again." Ana
begins fussing around her and fixing the blankets and pillows
to Enca's annoyance "Si, we have the crib, the blankets and
the clothes. We boiled the linens for the new one just like
you said and dried them in the midday sun. We oiled the
cradle and cleaned the baby's place like for a prince!"
"Si everything else," Enca talks to Maria directly, "pero...."

Her aunt hates to be interrupted and bursts out at
her niece. "Now is not the time to ask questions, mija! My
niece is so smart. But she doesn't realize that it is better to
know how to answer questions the right way eh? Like when a
man asks you a certain question and you should say NO!"

Shouting back, Enca is holding her belly, "What's
done is done, *mija* tia, and as you see is about to come!"

Sensing an old argument, Maria takes charge and stops
both women by holding up her hands. "Por *favor*. For the
next few hours we must work together. Escuchame?"

Contrite, they both back down and seem to be more at
ease. Recovered, Enca begins her questions again.
"Señora, I know you went to school back in your country
before you came here."
Tia answers for her, "she went to school in Palermo, Italy, a

university."

Maria laughs, "Ana, I am surprised you remember that." "Señora, when you spend as many hours together as you and I have delivering my four sons, you remember the talk so you forget the rest!"
Enca sounding hopeful, "so you are Italian?"
Maria busies her self checking the mother again and chatting easily.

"The University of Palermo is in Sicily. If you ask where I am from, I will say Italy. If you ask what I am, I will tell you Sicilian. But you were both right. I was fortunate to be one of the first women to take my learning there, even though sometimes I had to keep my chair outside the doors of some professori who would not accept a woman to study medicine. But my grandmother and her mother before her had always been midwifes, and I was proud to continue their work."

Ana, 'our grandfather called the midwife, Bruja, a witch."

Maria, "Si, in Sicily we are Strega. But that is only until their wives are screaming and their new son is turning blue. Then they call the midwife, please come please come."
All three laugh and join in the joke, "Then it was Santa Strega."
"Holy Bruja." Maria, finished checking and sits again beside the bed. "Then when the children are gown and behaving badly, the mother say, "Damn that midwife that pulled your feet out!"
"Enca, my father always says that the baby inside the mama knows all wisdom. But being born is so hard they forget everything." She lumbers up and begins to move around the room. "Enca" stay put, her aunt fusses, walking right behind her. "Your father certainly proved how much men have to learn."
Maria adds, "and women have not found any new ways to bring these children into the world.
Enca doubles over in pain and lays back down. Her

aunt holds her hand and covers her head with a damp cloth. A few minutes later Enca stubbornly goes back to her questions. "Pero, Señora Maria, writing down my favorite prayer, olive oil, my man's knife, tea and chocolate. These things speak to me of the tales the old women tell, not what a modern doctore would ask for."

Maria sits down next to Enca, "and my child having a child, do you find no wisdom in the old ways?"
Ana replies for her again, "she does! You know you throw the bucket of water out the window for New Year's luck!"
"Si, Tia, but everyone does that! I just thought since Maria went to university..."
"What, she would be wiser than your Abuleta?"
Maria speaks quietly, all the while gently massaging the young mother's limbs. "I went to university run by men, so I would be official and they would respect me. But what I know best, that I learned at the sides of many, many women. I helped my first mother when I was only 15. My grandmother chose me of all her grandchildren. I stayed when my mother was having my youngest brother. All the others had run away. I held my mother's hand and my grandmother saw I had the calling."

Enca is not convinced. She wants more assurances so Maria gives them to her. "It was the nurses the first taught doctors in the woman's hospital wards to wash their filthy hands before moving onto the next poor mother. They were killing women faster than their precious cattle."

Ana pipes up, "Florence Nightingale saved more lives with soap than all the doctors on the battlefields of Europe." The other women look at her in surprise. "Señora, I remember when you worked hard to get your papers here in the States. When I was having my second one, Manolito, you brought all your books to read to me, just like a Lector!"

"Thank you Ana, for helping me with that. The State of Florida gave me a certificate, but it is the mothers who give me their trust. If we have danger, we call a doctor. If not, we do what women have always done."

"So niece, you do know the knife under the pillow is to cut your pain." Enca feels another contraction coming on and asks hopefully, "do you think it works?"

Ana sits next to her in the bed and leans Enca against her larger, soft body. "Listen, *mi amorcita*. I have a story. There was a little girl who was afraid to go to sleep at night. Her parents tried to talk her out of her fears, but nothing helped. Until her abuela showed her a magic coin, She told her it was very old, a family treasure. She placed this coin under the girl's mattress and told her that as long as it was there nothing could harm her and she would be safe. The little girl slept like the sweet angel she was that night and every night after." Then, she leans back on the pillow, savoring her own memory. "And, do you know who that little girl was? Enca closes her eyes, peaceful, "You never told me that story before."
And, you tell me everything?"

Another pain hits Enca and she gives off a string of curses in Spanish, "*Jesu Cristo! Ay Carajo! Come mierda!* Ana tries to calm her, "Mija! Jesus will not help you if you curse at him!"

Maria steps in, "Let her go. She must help this baby to come in any way she can. "It hurts so much! Will each pain be worse and worse?"
Ana comforts her, softly answering, "Only until the best of all things happens."

Maria examines Enca as the pain passes. "Now, we are going to need the olive oil. You cook with olive oil, no, Enca?" "Si, Señora Maria, how can you cook without it?" Now she is talking about something she really knows and she sits up in the bed, alert and engaged. "No sofrito, no platanos, even rice and eggs needs a little drop of oil. You don't cook nothin' without some good Spanish olive oil. You think I cook like an American with Crisco? *Dios mio,* my father would walk out if I put that on the table."
Ana laughs, "Like the spaghetti you made that time. Remember, Papa couldn't even get in on his fork."

"Si, si, which is why I massage you with the oil you use every day. Your baby has been tasting your cooking for nine months now. If I used my Italian oil to rub you down, your baby would think she was coming to the wrong house!"

Enca is hit with another contraction. "Maria, Ana, it hurts so bad, he is killing me!"

"I know my pet. Be brave for your baby, for your child. You don't want fear to be his first knowing of his mother do you?"

Ana is helpless with worry now and responds with anger. "Well, you could have gone to *Centro Austuriano* and had the twilight sleep. *Como una Amerciana!*

Enca defiant even in pain. "He wanted me to. He set it all up, like he sets everything up. But I want to have my precious one at home, not surrounded by strangers asking a lot of stupid questions. This is why I am so glad to be with you, Señora."

Ana whispers to Maria! "He is a bastard!"

Maria nods and turns away, adding "If I took the time to pass judgement on the mothers I serve, I would not have time to birth their babies." Maria speaks in a soft voice. "Every life is a new beginning. We bring your child into this world. Then, I will write your names in my diary. In Sicily, we have birth records going back 500 years. Today, I add your name, Señorita Encarnaction."

Enca says with quiet pride, "It is Señora now."

Ana is beside herself, "He married you! Why didn't you tell me? When? In the church? Oh thank God, now your child has a father and can have a name in this town."

The grown woman inside Enca shows up,

"I married him! We went to Miami because he was in a big hurry all of a sudden. He has an uncle there who is a priest. And my son would always have a name, the name I give him, or the name she makes for herself in this world!"

From under the blankets, Maria lifts her head out to say,

"And, you will have this new citizen very soon, I think."

Enca lies back after her outburst. "I am so tired!"

Maria and Ana smile, "If you think you are tired now,
Just wait until you hear that sweet little cry in the middle of
the night and in the early morning, "Mama!"
"Ana, now would be a good time for some of that tea."
Enca, petulantly snaps "I don't want any tea, I drink *café*.
What am I English?"
Maria is firm, "Cool chamomile tea with honey for Mammi
here to sip and *café* for me and you Ana, please.
Enca is thoughtful when Ana leaves the room.
"You said, my son."
"Si"
"How do you know?"
"I know because you told me."
"I told you when?"
"When you cried out, *He* is killing me!"

      Ana walks in with a tray. "A boy, I knew it. I could
tell by the way she carried him so low. Boys always ride low
and try to show mama who is boss by twisting and kicking.
Girls sit high, close the mama's heart, where she will always
rest."

      "Now who is telling the old woman's tales?
Aye! Carajo!" A new pain hits and women move into action,
Ana by Enca's head and Maria between her legs. Ana turns
to Maria to distract herself. "Señora, why the chocolate?"
Maria smiles, "Because when I bring two or three or even
four babies into the world in one day, I need my favorite
treat! Now, Sweet mommi, now is the time you will begin to
push. Here we will say your favorite prayer; it is my favorite
as well. The mother of Jesus learned what pain was from her
blessed Son. She will comfort her daughters."
All three begin to recite the Hail Mary. Enca says it in
English, Maria in Italian and Ana in Spanish.

Hail Mary full of Grace
The Lord is with thee
Blessed are thou among women
And blessed is the fruit of thy womb Jesus

Ave Maria, gratia plena,
Dominus tecum,
benedicta tu in mulieribus,
et benedictus fructus ventris tui Iesus.

Santa Maria Madre di Dio,
María, llena eres de gracia,
el Señor es contigo.
Bendita tú eres entre todas las mujeres,
y bendito es el fruto de tu vientre, Jesús. carnacion!
Beddo bambino!

    Later Maria leaves the new mother with her babe in arms, Ana finally quiet beside her. She drives across Ybor in the dusk of the same day and returns to her desk to write of this child's arrival.

    Maria Messina Greco was born in 1878 in Mirabella, Sicily. At the age of 18 she was one of the first women to study at the University of Palermo. She was one of the first women to study at any university in Europe. She received her degree in Midwifery. During her time in Italy she delivered 2,000   children.

    In 1904 at the age of 26, she came to the United States to a marriage with Salvatore C. Greco. They soon moved from his parent's home up the street to what would be their home for the next 30 years: 1828 Seventh Avenue, Ybor   City.

    Maria began her midwife service soon after arriving in the States and wrote each birth in her diary.
6,734 were recorded in these small books.

    In 1930 Maria retired and she and her husband went to live with their only child, Delia Spoto. They had one grandson, Dr. Joseph A., Spoto, Jr. and lived in Redington Beach. In August of 1957, Salvatore died.

    Less than one year later, Maria wrote her daughter complete instructions for her burial. (in Italian) and left it on her nightstand. She asked to be buried in her husband's favorite dress. Then Maria Messina Greco, the woman who had brought so many lives into the world, quietly filled an apron with rocks and walked into the Gulf of Mexico. She left her shoes and jewelry folded neatly on the shore. She was 78 years old and had brought 12,000 new people into this life.

The Busker

The young man makes his way down the sidewalk, weaving through the crowds strolling down the brick streets. The smell of Cuban coffee and cigar smoke drifts out to him from the shops as he passes. He stops at the corner, deciding which way to go, leans his case against the antique street lamp and looks up at the decorative sign, *La Septima*, "That means Seven," he thinks; "that's Good luck!" Looking around for a place that seems right, he avoids the tattoo parlors, vintage clothes stores and head shops and settles on a quiet little corner across from an old movie house. He puts down his case, opens it and throws in a couple of dollars for his *seed money*. He checks his tuning, keeps his head down waiting for the right moment, takes a deep breath and begins to play, tentative at first, then growing surer and finally, standing tall with his head back, begins to sing.

People pass, look; some stop to listen for a bit; others can't be bothered. A big guy stops for a second, nodding in time to the music, drops a couple of bucks in the case, smiles and walks off. Sweet! He thinks. Broke the ice! And, it seems like it did. More folks are stopping to listen and most are donating to the cause. A young policeman walking the beat pauses and listens for a whole song, then comments, "That was nice, man, very nice."

"Thanks buddy," he responds and then wishes he hadn't said it. The policeman is giving him an appraising look. "You wrote that didn't you?" he asks.

"Yeah, I did."

"You could tell." the officer replies, "It was very personal, *fresh*."

"Thanks", he says. The officer gives out a little sigh… "Uh, speaking of personal, could I see your ID, please." Uh oh, here it comes. The cop studies the ID, holds it up next to his face. Smiles and nods, "Well, that's you, all right. I know that name. You come from a talented family

He's a little surprised but smiles and answers, "Sure do!"

"Your mother *and* your father," the policeman adds.

"Thanks, yeah. They both have been playing for a lot of years. Then, they decided to settle down and have a family, which worked out pretty good for me."

The cop looks up and down the street, making up his mind, "OK, son, the problem is you are right out here in the open; you're on Broadway, man! If someone sees you and complains and my captain finds out, he would have my ass."

"Got it," He answers and starts to pack up. "Listen," the cop adds, "There are lots of other good places, you just got to know where to go. First thing you need to do is get off 7th avenue. Go down a couple blocks to 15th St. There's a great place, with lots of people walking by, heading to the restaurants; it's close to the campus; I think you would do good there; they'll enjoy your music. Give it a shot. Otherwise, I'll have to give you a citation."

"A citation," he answers playing the kid…that's good, right? No, it's not," the cop chuckles, "but, I get the feeling you already knew that." Relieved, the Busker says, "Hey, thanks a lot, man, I appreciate it. No problem, let me just get my stuff." "Gotta tell you that song was great and you play well, too. You take lessons?"

"Naw, I did for a while but I just wasn't feeling' it."
The policeman pauses a moment looking down at him, then
comments, "Do yourself a favor and look up Open Tuning.
You tune the guitar so that a strum across the strings plays a
full chord. That's where Keith Richards keeps all his money.
It'll make it easier for you and then you can experiment with
some tonal effects, too. Give it a try."

Obviously impressed, he asks, "Are you in a band or
something?" "Yeah," the cop chuckles. "The uniform fools
everybody. Well, I was. I had plans but that's all behind me,
now. I'm just trying to keep the peace these days."

"Well, that's a shame, because you got something
real to offer people, you know?" If you don't mind me
asking, what happened, man?"
"Life happened "the Officer answers. What can I say? Life is
what happens while you're busy making other plans. You
know who said that?"
The kid nods his head, "John Lennon." "Well, you sure have
been taught well," the officer replies then adds, "Here let me
help you out and good luck to you!" as he throws some bills
in the case.

The busker can't help but feel that what just
happened can't be your everyday thing as he watches the
officer walk away. So, he cuts across the campus lugging his
case and smiling at the girls that pass by. I like this already, he
thinks, as he settles in a new location, sets himself up and
begins to sing. He feels good, the cop really made his day. A
couple of young girls pass, giving him a quick look and then,
one with full arm sleeve says loudly.
"Oh look, it's a hippie! Whipping Post!" she catcalls. Her
friend, watching the busker, is bothered by this distraction,
says "I am trying to listen here. Please, chill."

"Chill shit!" Sleeves cracks and her friend sighs,
"Don't be a bore! I want to listen." We have got to go,"
Sleeves is getting louder. "That Castle guy's not going to wait
forever." "He'll wait," her friend assures her. "We got plenty
of time. This guy's cute… and he's good!"

"Yeah, he's cute, he's good, can we go now? Damn!"

"You are really good!" she smiles and nods at the Busker, then turns to her friend, "C'mon, let me listen to him."

Breaking from the song, he says, "Come on, let her stay."

Sleeves scoffs, "What, you think she's here for you? Oh, please. I am not gonna stand here on the street listening to this guy. I got shit to do!" Turning to leave she throws over her shoulder, "It's not worth it dude; she is just going to *play* you!"

The Busker finishes his song to polite applause; the friendly girl comments, beaming. "Kool! You're like the guy from *Once*. I love that. Do you know it?"

"The music from *Once*?" he asks, "Yeah!" She answers. "Sure!" He replies. "You wanna do it?" She flirts. He answers, cautiously, "The song?" "Yeah, the song, silly. You and me." The Busker's surprised but shrugs "All right."

He plays the opening and people are starting to gather. When she joins in after the first verse, he can't help but smile at their harmonizing. They build to full voice near the end, and he lets her have the moment and then ends, strumming as they hit all the high notes, looking at each other in wonder at how good it is.

The crowd loves it! They respond generously. Blushing and nodding at the applause, she turns to him, coolly adding and "Nailed it in one take!"

Ruining the moment, Sleeves shows up again; "Girl, what do you think you are doing? Are you coming or not?'

"I always have to drag your ass around; I'm sick of your shit. You call me up, you want to go out; I call the Castle guy; I set it up, and I pick you up. You end up hanging around the damn street watching a dude play guitar!"
"Whaddya know? There goes Miriam playing the bitch again. Give us some space, please. We've got something going on," she tells her.

We? You don't even know his name! Dude, does she know your name?"

"Not yet," he replies. Then she asks him, "do you know her name?"

"Goodbye, Miriam," the girl says. So that's Sleeve's name.

"What, am I dismissed, now? Oh, pardon me, kind sir, I must be away!" They breathe a sigh of relief as she leaves.

The girl turns to the Busker, "We were good," she says shyly. Nodding, he agrees, "Yeah, we were. We should do more," she adds. "Yeah, we should. Like, a lot more," she coos moving closer. "I like a lot," the Busker nods, smiling. "Well, what's your night like?" she asks. "You going to be here all night? It's up to me. I usually stay for a while. it's always nice to fill up the case."

"Oh, the case! Shit I forgot all about it! Now I have no way to get into the club!"

"I'm sorry" he says…but I'm still glad you stayed. Yeah, she agrees, "Totally; me too. What was your name again?" Jon, he answers, "Yours?"

"Katie. Jon, it was so great meeting you. I dug your music and I'd like to spend some more time with you. But, right now, I've really got to go. Unfortunately, she's my ride and… But I can come back. Would you like that? If, I came back?" "Yeah," he replies, "I'd like that." "Then I will come back," she affirms. "Sweetness," he responds. "You can tell, huh? Oh my god! I just remembered. How the hell am I going to get in? I lost my way in"! Distraught, she looks around then down at his case. "If I could just get in, I'd be ok. Then, at least, I'd have my ride and I could still come by later. I would pay you back." They stand facing each other for an awkward moment, then making up his mind the Busker gestures at the case, "Take what you need." Katie begins to babble gratefully as she takes the money from his case. "Oh Jon, you are a lifesaver! I'm so glad I met you and loved singing together. I can't wait to do it again. I'll come back, I will be back. It'll be later but I will be back." She kisses him on the cheek, turns to walk away, and then stops to ask, "You will wait, won't you?"

The Busker does the strong silent thing and starts playing again, very slowly. He notices Miriam in the back of the crowd. Later, they stand apart looking at each other. There is a silent moment between them. With a shake of her head, she says "I tried to warn you, bro," as she turns away.

The Busker looks up and around, makes up his mind and begins to collect his stuff to go. Just then, a couple walks up; "You're not leaving, are you? We were just listening from across the street; you were so great!"

The older woman gushes, "Don't go yet; play another song!" Her husband seemed just as enthused. Looking at their warm smiles, how could he resist? "You got it, guys!"

Packing his stuff at the end of the night he muses, all in all not a bad evening, considering how it started. Oh, well, what the hell, he thinks, heading to his car. As he passes Theatre Ybor, he hears something from the bushes. He listens for a second, shrugs and moves on. Then there is a distinctive "Hey!" from the bushes. Cautiously, he approaches, trying to see who is calling out. Then, a woman's voice slurring, "Nice guy leaving me cause I'm drunk." "Did I hear that right?" He thinks, "What the hell? Who's there?" he calls. "It's me, Katie! You're just leaving me here?" He approaches, asking "What are you doing there? Then, the distinctive sound of someone being sick in the bushes answers his question. "Why don't you come out of there?" He says. "I can't," she replies. Parting the branches, he sees something slumped against the wall of the building, "Do you need help?" "No, I'm fine here," she mumbles. He moves to help her up and out.

She's a mess, mumbling and crying and making no sense. "Do you have someone to help you get home?"

"Yeah," she says, "You?" The Busker thinks it over, "OK, sit tight. I'll get my car and come back to pick you up." "OK," she answers, crying again. "You'll be ok." He tries to console her. "Really?" she replies, I don't see how." Look at me!" "Don't worry; I'll be back in 15 minutes." "OK," she slurs again. As he makes his way out of the bushes, she calls out to him, "The money's all gone, you know." "Just sit tight, he says. "I'll be right back for you. "Really? for me?" She asks, sounding like a little girl. "Really." he says and he's off.

"Wait! Wait," she cries out. "Jon! Wait!" "OK," he answers, "I'm coming!" What is it?

"Why are you doing all this for me?" Why?" he asks, "Cause I'm stupid."

Two hours later, the Busker returns home, guitar case in hand, feeling not like he expected to feel, at all. His mom is the first to greet him, "Aha, our busker has come home! How did it go?" "Not too bad," he replies. With her hands on his shoulders, she looks into her son's eyes, searching. "Well you are now part of a long line of artists, musicians, actors and jugglers going back hundreds, if not even thousands of years. I am so proud of you," as she hugs her young one.

"Where's Pops?" he wants to know. "He's around; he'll be so glad to hear you're back, safe and sound." "Be in my room," as he maneuvers his case down the narrow hall. He flops on the still unmade bed, kicks his shoes off and lies back with his hands behind his head, staring at the ceiling, then, just as quickly sits up and grabs his case and takes out the guitar. Slowly strumming, he sings some of his favorites, muses for a moment and begins carefully strumming out some of what the cop had told him.

Dad pauses in the doorway listening, "Something new?"
"Just noodling," he smiles; it's one of their shared expressions.
"How was it?"
"Pretty sweet," I guess." Nodding his head, the dad asks, "Where'd you go?"
"A couple of places." Grinning, the dad wants to know, "Make any money?"

105

"Some. Not too much."
Starting to turn away, his father adds, "Some of the best times I ever had playing were for not too much. "Yeah," Jon nods adding, "The cop knew about you guys, heard you play."
The father's smile slides off his face, "The cop!" Yeah, nice guy gave me some ideas of places to play.
Dad being a dad says "I have to ask, How in the hell did he know who you were?"
"I, uh, told him when he complimented my playing. He even taught me something cool on my guitar."
Like what?" Dad wants to know.
"Open tuning, you know about that?"
"Your mom uses it, some." "Figures," says Jon.
He kind of blew me away! Jon grins and, not just with the music."
"Hey Hon, the cop knew who we were." Mom peeks around the open doorway, "Say that again, slowly."
"It's all good!" Dad jokes, "Our son got away with it." "OK, that's it! No supper for either of you tonight!" as she heads back to the kitchen.

Father and son share a laugh, as the dad turns to leave, his son takes a deep breath and asks, "Hey, Pops, have you ever known somebody that you thought was a...? After a beat, Dad asks, "A what, son?"

"Somebody, that you didn't know whether you were nothin', never mind."
Dad waits looking down fondly, "You sure, boy?"
"Yeah. No biggie," His son answers.
"All right, but if you change your mind, you know where I'm at."
"Sweetness," he responds as he picks up his guitar and begins strumming and singing, one of his mom's songs..

NEBRASKA AVENUE
Maggie Council DiPietra

On our street
We got historic bungalows
On our street
We got porn shops and hoes
At the Pakistani drive thru
Where we go for cigs and beer
The artists and the homeless
And the Yuppie pioneers
There seems to be room for all
Down on Nebraska Avenue
And the people go
Boing boing boing boing

Home

There are over 20 cemeteries in proximity to Ybor City with many more radiating out from the central hub.

Tampeños like to keep their loved ones close. There are sprawling acres of lush manicured greenery like Garden of Memories, where most of my family rests, and small neighborhood graveyards, as well as others that are private and gated like L'Unione Italiano.

Ybor even has two of its own sites that are part of the National Register of Historic Places. They were public cemeteries, open to all. Confederate soldiers, pirates and slaves, mobsters, priests and nuns all rest there, as well as the great Vincente de Ybor, himself.

One way or another, they all ended up here, in our town.

As I drive the brick streets of Ybor on this beautiful evening, I feel so at ease in knowing this place will always be here. And, unlike most everything else, will not change, especially the parts of it we love so much.

Ybor City is Historic. Much of it cannot be changed. You are always going to be able to take the drive down La

Septima and smell the cigar smoke and food cooking. You can stroll along the shops with the flagstone sidewalks that have the names of people etched into the stone. People who loved living here, raised their families here and wanted it known that they, too had walked the same path.

I Remember Tampa
Mike Baluja

I remember Tampa the way she used to be
The places we would run to, the face we would see
A city rising on the move, A simple, yet, progressive groove
I remember Tampa, and she remembers me…
With love that I could call my own
A love that I have always known
This city that I call my home
The home from which I'll never roam
This love affair was meant to be
 I love her and she loves me
Yes, I remember Tampa, and she remembers me…

Lyrics Credits

"I remember Tampa" by Mike Baluja
@c 2012 Mb Sounds/Mike Baluja
All Rights Reserved. Used by Permission

"Nebraska Avenue" by Maggie Council DiPietra
@c2008 /created with support by the Arts Council of
Hillsborough County & Board of Commissioners
All Rights Reserved. Used by Permission

Mosquito by Ray Villadonga
@c2015 Mystic Baboon Publishing
 admin by Lorena Villadonga Bacus

ABOUT THE AUTHORS

Mary Ellen & Richard DiPietra

The DiPietra's began their collaboration with cohabitation in Hell's Kitchen, NYC in 1981. Thirty-five years of marriage later, a wonderful son, Nick, several plays and now they have written their first book. *I am a Cuban Sandwich* first came to life as a one-man show, which they produced over 30 times in theaters in Florida and NY. Then came the *Ybor Stories,* with 15 amazing actors, musicians and crew. The premier performance took place in a former cigar factory, the site of El Lector.

They hope this is just the beginning. They have many more tales to share.

Please follow us on Facebook at:

I am A Cuban Sandwich

email: IamaCubanSandwich9@gmail.com

Do tell us your tales of Ybor or your hometown!

Please Buy our book on Amazon.com

And hopefully someday at bookstore near you!

Made in the USA
Las Vegas, NV
16 September 2022

55392227R00067